ammam
mc
Manama

Doha

Dubai

Abu Dhabi

Muscat

RUB 'AL-KHALI

DHUFAR

Salalah

ARABIAN PENINSULA

SAUDI ARABIA

KUWAIT

BAHRAIN

QATAR

UNITED ARAB EMIRATES

OMAN

NORTH YEMEN

SOUTH YEMEN

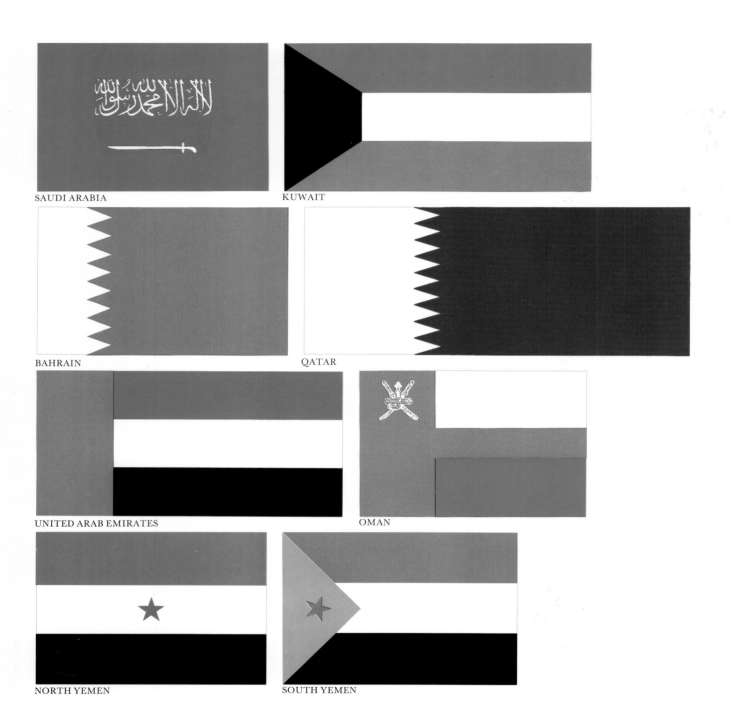

SAUDI ARABIA

KUWAIT

BAHRAIN

QATAR

UNITED ARAB EMIRATES

OMAN

NORTH YEMEN

SOUTH YEMEN

ARABIAN PENINSULA

By the Editors of Time-Life Books
With photographs by Pascal and Maria Maréchaux

TIME-LIFE BOOKS · AMSTERDAM

TIME-LIFE BOOKS

EUROPEAN EDITOR: Ellen Phillips
Design Director: Ed Skyner
Director of Editorial Resources: Samantha Hill
Chief Sub-Editor: Ilse Gray

LIBRARY OF NATIONS

Series Director: Dale M. Brown
Designer: Thomas S. Huestis

Editorial Staff for *Arabian Peninsula*
Associate Editors: Roberta Conlan, Jim Hicks, Anne Horan
(text), Jane Speicher Jordan (pictures)
Researchers: Paula York-Soderlund (principal), Karin
Kinney, Rita Thievon Mullin
Assistant Designers: Robert K. Herndon, Mary Staples
Sub-Editor: Sally Rowland
Copy Co-ordinators: Margery du Mond, Robert M. S.
Somerville
Picture Co-ordinator: Erin Monroney
Editorial Assistant: Myrna E. Traylor

EDITORIAL PRODUCTION FOR THE SERIES

Chief: Ellen Brush
Traffic Co-ordinators: Jane Lillicrap, Rosalind Munro
Editorial Department: Theresa John, Debra Lelliott,
Sylvia Osborne

Correspondents: Elisabeth Kraemer (Bonn); Margot
Hapgood, Dorothy Bacon (London); Miriam Hsia, Lucy
T. Voulgaris (New York); Maria Vincenza Aloisi,
Josephine du Brusle (Paris); Ann Natanson (Rome).

ISBN 0 7054 0851 5

TIME-LIFE is a trademark of Time Warner Inc. U.S.A.

CONSULTANTS: Chapter 1: Dr. Gusvan Beek,
curator of Old World archaeology at the
Smithsonian Institution in Washington D.C. has
done archaeological field work in North and South
Yemen and in southern Saudi Arabia. Chapter 2:
Dr. John Esposito, Chairman of the Department of
Religious Studies at The College of The Holy
Cross in Worcester, Massachusetts, has written
extensively about Islam. Chapter 3: Dr. Federico
S. Vidal, a member of the Department of
Sociology, Anthropology and Social Work at the
University of Texas at Arlington, is a specialist in
the culture of the nomadic Bedouin of the Arabian
Peninsula. Chapter 4: John F. Mason, a retired
geologist devoted 40 years of his career to oil
exploration, some of it conducted in the Middle
East. Dr. Curtis Larsen, also a geologist, has
extensive knowledge of the hydrology of the
Arabian Peninsula. Chapters 5 and 6: Dr. David
Long, a member of the United States Foreign
Service, specializes in Arab affairs.

PHOTOGRAPHERS: Pascal and Maria
Maréchaux are architects as well as
photographers. Pascal made his first trip to the
Arabian Peninsula in 1975. His book on Yemen,
Arabia Felix, has been published in Europe and the
United States. The Maréchaux spent four weeks
travelling in Saudi Arabia for this volume.

Special Contributors: The chapter texts were written
by: Ron Bailey, Anne Horan, John Neary, Milton
Orshefsky and Bryce Walker.
Other Contributor: Rosemary George.

Cover: The television broadcasting building of the
Ministry of Information in Riyadh symbolizes the
new Saudi Arabia, a kingdom that developed in
just half a century from a poor desert tribal society
into one of the world's wealthiest nations. The
building was designed by a French architect.

Front and back endpapers: Bounded on the east
by the Arabian Gulf, on the south by the Arabian
Sea and on the west by the Red Sea, the Arabian
Peninsula encompasses more than 2 million
square kilometres of mountains and desert. A land
without rivers, it has wadis instead—dried
streambeds that flow with water only after rare
rainstorms.

This volume is one in a series of books describing
countries of the world—their natural resources, peoples,
histories, economies and governments.

CONTENTS

Two citizens of Dubai eat while watching ice hockey at a local 1,500-seat rink. Throughout the Arabian Peninsula, oil-rich businessmen, eager to

modernize their countries, are pouring billions of dollars into lavish sports facilities. Their ultimate goal: to host the Olympic Games.

REALMS OF SAND

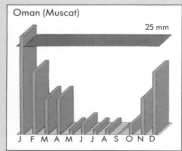

Kuwait (Kuwait)
25 mm
J F M A M J J A S O N D

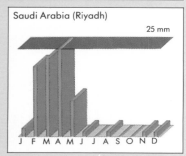

Oman (Muscat)
25 mm
J F M A M J J A S O N D

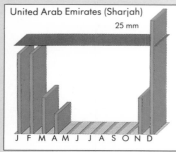

Saudi Arabia (Riyadh)
25 mm
J F M A M J J A S O N D

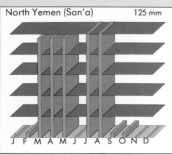

United Arab Emirates (Sharjah)
25 mm
J F M A M J J A S O N D

North Yemen (San'a)
125 mm
J F M A M J J A S O N D

One of the world's most arid regions, the Arabian Peninsula contains three major deserts–the Great Nafud, the Dahna and the Rub'al-Khali, or Empty Quarter. The Great Nafud in the north encompasses 65,000 square kilometres and is made up of longitudinal dunes that extend many kilometres and soar to heights of 90 metres. Stretching south from the Great Nafud is the 640-kilometre-long Dahna, a narrow strip of sand dunes. The Dahna's southern tip joins with the Rub'al-Khali, which blankets more than 650,000 square kilometres. Here, sand mountains climb as high as 300 metres.

The temperature in all three deserts averages 44°C in the summer and often rises to 54°C. The little rain that falls *(graphs, left)* is quickly absorbed by the parched sand of the deserts and the gravelly areas found throughout most of the rest of the peninsula.

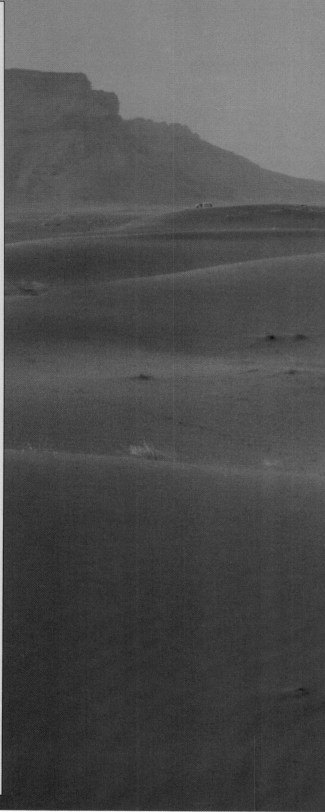

In south-western Saudi Arabia, a lone Bedouin strides a bleak desert track near the border with North Yemen.

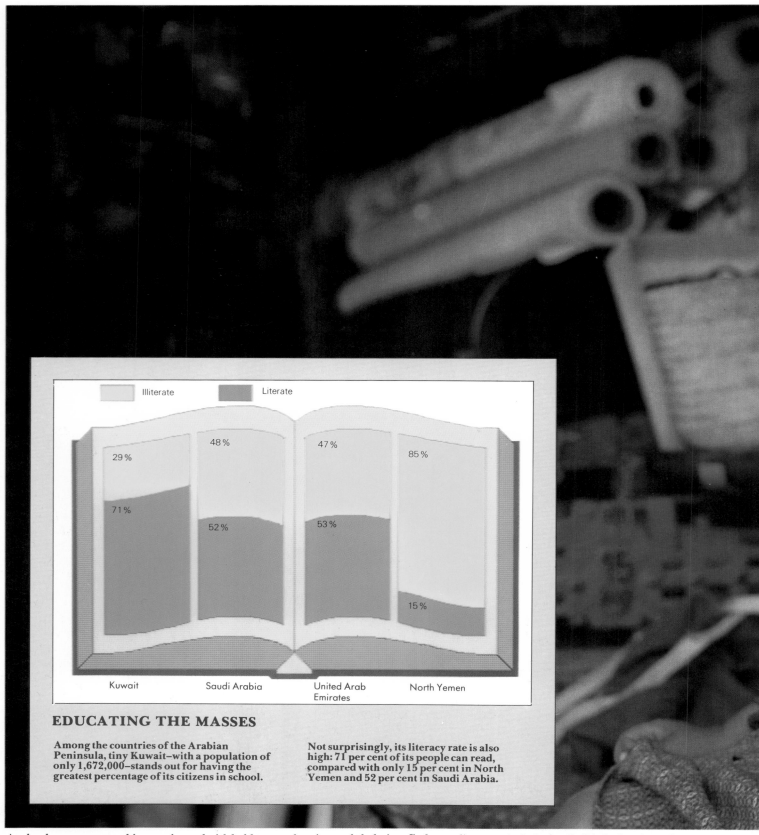

Illiterate	Literate

Kuwait	Saudi Arabia	United Arab Emirates	North Yemen
29 %	48 %	47 %	85 %
71 %	52 %	53 %	15 %

EDUCATING THE MASSES

Among the countries of the Arabian Peninsula, tiny Kuwait–with a population of only 1,672,000–stands out for having the greatest percentage of its citizens in school.

Not surprisingly, its literacy rate is also high: 71 per cent of its people can read, compared with only 15 per cent in North Yemen and 52 per cent in Saudi Arabia.

A school-age youngster, his eyes rimmed with kohl to guard against ophthalmia, a fly-borne disease, minds the family fabric shop in Saafan, North

Yemen. More than 400,000 of the country's children now attend primary schools, but the student-teacher ratio is close to 40 to 1.

11

WHERE THE OIL IS

Of the 10 countries with the largest proven oil reserves, three–Saudi Arabia, Kuwait and Abu Dhabi–lie on the Arabian Peninsula. Saudi Arabia, with approximately 170 billion barrels, accounts for a quarter of the world total.

At Ras Tanura, site of Saudi Arabia's largest refinery, crude oil is processed at a rate exceeding 400,000 barrels a day. In the early 1980s, Saudi Arabia

was exporting more than two billion barrels a year–nearly 98 per cent of its annual production.

OBJECT OF THE PILGRIMS' DESIRE

The world's largest religious gathering takes place annually in the ancient Saudi Arabian city of Mecca. Here, hundreds of thousands of pilgrims assemble from as far away as Afghanistan and Uganda, India and Malaysia to complete the *hajj* or Great Pilgrimage. Three quarters of the foreign visitors arrive by air; 20 years ago only 18 per cent did.

In the early years of the Saudi kingdom, taxes levied on the faithful were a major source of government revenue. But with the advent of new riches based on oil, the tax was abolished. By the mid-1970s, the Saudi government was instead spending the equivalent of $50 million a year to accommodate the influx of pilgrims, receiving only a fraction in return.

Muslims from all over the world converge on the slopes of Mount Arafat as the climax to the annual Great Pilgrimage to Mecca. Many of them carry umbrellas

for protection against the intense heat.

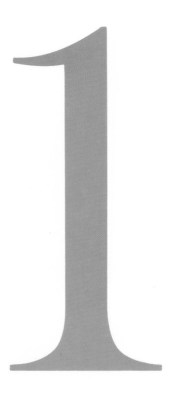

Towers of stone and brick rise above
the streets of old San'a, capital of
North Yemen. The city—whose name
means "beautifully built"—is sited on a
2,300-metre-high plain.

OIL-RICH LANDS OF DESTINY

In the last week of April 1939, King Abd al-Aziz ibn Saud set out from his capital at Riyadh in central Arabia on an historic journey. Accompanying him were a party of 2,000 travellers—his elder sons; brothers and cousins; some of his wives and concubines; hundreds upon hundreds of soldiers and servants; and a handful of American businessmen representing an Arabian and American consortium formed six years before to prospect for minerals, oil and water. The travellers were bound for the gravel and rock-strewn plains along the coast of the Arabian Gulf, 400 kilometres to the east, so that the King could preside over the dispatch westwards of oil that had finally been drawn from the earth after years of near-hopeless drilling.

Travelling in a single file of 500 cars, the caravan covered about 80 kilometres a day, hardly more than a camel's pace. Trucks brought up the rear, carrying some 350 white canvas tents and the Persian carpets and silk cushions with which to adorn them, as well as scores of bleating sheep and cauldrons large enough to boil them whole.

King Ibn Saud and his party inched eastwards over an ancient trade route. There was little to see in the way of landmarks, only the rutted trail to suggest a bygone human presence and, at wide intervals, a well and perhaps a few tents camped nearby.

By long-established desert code, certain Bedouin tribes had pasturing and watering rights at certain wells; and on the approach of the King's caravan, the regional Bedouin chief and a band of his male kin would come out to welcome the royal traveller, greet him with a litany of salutations and proffer brass-studded bowls of salty-tasting camel's milk for him and his companions to drink. The King gave them such gifts as woollen cloaks and silver coins in exchange and made them welcome at the next meal that his minions spread out on the desert sand.

Between wells, no paved roads sped the cars along, and no signposts guided the way; the King's caravan charted its course, as his Arabian forebears had done for two or three millennia, by the position of the stars at night and by a certain homing instinct.

Nor were there any hotels to provide bed and board *en route*. When the party halted for food and rest, the King's retainers pitched the 350 tents with an alacrity that made it seem to one of the Americans in the party as if Aladdin had summoned them into being by rubbing his magic lamp. For food, the travellers feasted on fresh-slain sheep cooked in the great cauldrons that had been brought along. They quenched their thirst with tea and citrus fruits. And five times daily they performed their religious duty. The throng arranged itself in rows behind the King, who prostrated himself on the sand and led his subjects in prayer.

A week's travel took them across

1

about one third of the breadth of the Arabian Peninsula, to Ras Tanura, a sandspit on the Arabian Gulf, where a tanker was standing by. After a round of feasting and exchange of gifts–a Cadillac and a chest of gold coins for the King (representing payment due for the oil strike) and gold watches for the oilmen–the 1.9 metre tall Ibn Saud bent over a mammoth steel wheel connected to the pipelines and turned it with his own hand. A valve opened, sending the first trickle of Arabia's oil into the tanker that was to ferry the consignment off to the West.

In turning that industrial wheel the King had brought Saudi Arabia–and for all practical purposes the smaller states with which it shares the peninsula–to the dawn of a new era. During the few decades that have elapsed since then–a mere wink of time in that aeons-old land–an estimated 350 billion barrels' worth of subterranean oil has made the peninsula the world's major supplier of energy and consequently one of the richest and fastest-changing parts of the world.

The West has greeted the Arabians' sudden emergence on to the international stage with surprise. But the fact is that they played a leading role in international events twice before. The first time was a thousand-year epoch that lasted from biblical days to the decline of the Roman Empire, when they controlled the land route between the Mediterranean Sea and the Indian subcontinent and so became the middlemen of the world's commerce. "No race seems more prosperous," wrote the Byzantine scholar Photius, quoting a third-century B.C. Greek writer by the name of Ariston, "since they act as the warehouse for everything from Asia and Europe which goes

under the name of distinction."

Among the most highly prized of ancient trade commodities were two produced in Arabia itself–the exotic gum resins frankincense and myrrh. The New Testament chronicle of the Three Wise Men, who went to the Christ Child bearing gifts of myrrh, frankincense and gold, reflects the high value placed upon the two aromatics: they were considered to rank with gold, the most precious metal known to the ancient world, as appropriate gifts for a newborn king and redeemer. In Rome, frankincense and myrrh fetched such high prices that the Romans wrote enviously of the southern portion of the peninsula, where they were produced, as *Arabia Felix*–Arabia the Blessed.

The second epoch of wealth for the Arabians was the era of Muslim ascendancy, from early in the seventh century A.D. to late in the 15th, when the burgeoning of the Islamic faith combined with an explosion of religious, cultural and commercial energy to propel the Arabians out of their homeland and on to a path abroad. Islamic traders and warriors carried wealth, religion and learning east as far as Indonesia, west to Morocco and north from the Mediterranean to the Balkans, through Spain and on to the doorstep of France.

Now, the importance of oil to modern industry and modern living has thrust the Arabians into the limelight again. Between 1939 and 1981, the price of oil swelled from 10 cents a barrel to $32, bringing Saudi Arabia alone an annual income of $84 billion. Even with the lower oil prices of the mid-1980s, Saudi Arabia continues to prosper as the world's major oil supplier. With the money have come modern conveniences that were undreamt of before the peninsula's oil endow-

Portable tape recorders at the ready, Yemeni women in traditional garb–including brimmed straw hats–take part in a wedding celebration. All festivities are segregated by sex throughout most of the Arabian Peninsula.

1

ment was discovered. Macadamized roads have paved the ancient caravan routes. Concrete high-rise buildings have replaced mud-brick structures that used to stand at the desert cross-roads. Air conditioning cools homes and offices, machine-driven pumps draw water from subterranean reservoirs called aquifers, and desalination plants make sea water potable.

But the changes have been so fast-paced that age-old customs persist alongside the new, making the Arabian Peninsula a land of contrasts unique in the modern world. The car and pick-up truck have almost fully replaced the camel as a means of transport, but in the public markets they vie for parking space with sheep and goats, as they are still being raised for milk, wool and meat. The computer figures prominently in the merchant's counting-house—but offices and shops close five times daily so that everyone can pray. Some 550,000 young people, among them 155,000 women, annually attend local and foreign universities to bring their countries abreast of modern methods in science and engineering—in a society where robed men carry daggers, women wear veils and adultery is punished by public beheading with the sword.

One reason that ancient customs survive unchanged is that the Arabian Peninsula is so isolated from the rest of the world. Technically part of Asia, it is almost a subcontinent unto itself. It is the world's largest peninsula—a 3,048,000-square-kilometre tongue of land that is cut off from the rest of Asia by the Arabian (or Persian) Gulf on the east and by the vast Syrian desert on the north. It is separated from Africa by the Red Sea on the west. And on the south it is girt by the Gulf of Aden, the

JEWELS FROM THE FLOOR OF THE GULF

Wearing a bone noseclip, a diver surfaces with a basket of oysters.

In a tradition that dates back at least to 2000 B.C. and the ancient civilization of Dilmun, a dwindling cadre of men in the tiny island-state of Bahrain still pursues the harsh and dangerous occupation of diving for pearls in the Arabian Gulf.

As in the past, the divers shave their heads and wear black cotton shorts. On lung power alone (none of them use oxygen tanks), they dive as much as 25 metres below the surface, staying there for nearly two minutes. Each diver is paired with a *saib*, who remains on the dhow to haul the diver up at a signal on the weighted line. With only a lungful of air, a diver has little left to return to the surface, so his well-being depends on the strength and speed of his helper.

Arabian Sea and the Gulf of Oman—an arm and two fingers of the vast Indian Ocean.

The peninsula has a dearth of deep harbours to encourage seafaring and not a single river to provide interior transport and communication. Barely a third of the peninsula has arable fields to encourage farming—and those few fields are confined to the inland valleys of the mountains that rim the west and south coasts and to scattered oases of the desert interior.

This book is the story of the resourceful, enduring and enigmatic people who live in that forbidding land. They make up eight sovereign states—Kuwait, Bahrain, Qatar, the United Arab Emirates, Oman, and North and South Yemen as well as Saudi Arabia. All but the two Yemens—where oil has not yet been exploited—share in the emoluments of the modern oil age. And all share a common history. For most of them, that history has meant moving from oasis to oasis in search of water and pasturage, with intervals of settling down in times and places of plenty, and periods of the cultural flowering that accompanies settling down.

The perpetual motion of the people is reflected in the peninsula's very name. "Arabia" means "land of the Arabs", and "Arab" in turn is derived from a Semitic word that means "nomad". The first use of the term occurs in Assyrian annals of the ninth century B.C., when nomads mounted on camelback are reported to have raided the settled villages of Mesopotamia. Of the present population of 16 million, the majority are descended from the same stock as the Semitic people who took up a nomadic existence on the peninsula hundreds, perhaps even thousands, of years before that.

A small but fascinating group still clings to the nomadic way of life. The rest live in the oases and in coastal cities, where they farm, trade and engage in occupations that range from biochemistry and telecommunications to pushing for women's rights–pursuits that the oil wealth has opened up. But even today the lines between nomadic and settled folk tend to blur, for both groups mingle just as they have always mingled, and both honour the same values of righteousness, valour and hospitality–values born of the human struggle for survival in the desert.

The desert is one of the most brutal environments on earth. Daytime temperatures there often reach 55°C, and under the noon sun a flat rock surface is too hot to touch. Sudden winds of 100 kilometres an hour blow up at any time, causing swirling storms that fling dust and stones around the desert like shrapnel. In winter, after the sun goes down, the mercury dips below freezing-point. Years may go by before rain falls in any particular area, and then it comes as a violent downpour that turns dry gulleys into rampaging torrents. Afterwards, a thin tissue of grass sprouts and seemingly lifeless thorn trees send out tiny leaves–all that the desert grants in the way of pasturage.

The most desolate stretch of all is the enormous Rub'al-Khali, or Empty Quarter, which sprawls across much of the southern third of the peninsula and according to local folklore is the special haunt of jinns, demons and other evil

21

Columns of a temple built by the inhabitants of the kingdom of Saba more than 2,000 years ago cast long shadows across the sand near present day Ma'rib in North Yemen. Saba was the Sheba of the Bible.

spirits. A combination of great yellow-to-reddish dunes, some 150 metres high, and black shale outcrops, it constitutes an expanse roughly the size of France and contains, by one estimate, some 16,670 cubic kilometres of sand. This is the nomad's range land.

Arabia was not always the desiccated expanse that it is today. Thousands of years ago, glaciers covered much of the Northern Hemisphere. Spreading from the Arctic over most of Europe and south as far as the Anatolian plateau, the ice sheet generated cold, moist air that caused rain to fall on the Arabian Peninsula. Fresh-water lakes formed in the depressions, streams coursed down the slopes into rivers, grasses grew on the plains, and so did nut and berry-bearing shrubs, thereby setting the evolutionary stage for the arrival of foraging creatures.

By about 100,000 B.C., humans were roaming the land, gathering the nuts and berries and hunting aurochs and other prehistoric beasts. Where the human beings came from, nobody knows; but they left behind a wealth of stone axes and flint arrowheads.

About 17,000 years ago, desiccation set in. The rivers and lakes began to dry up, and the grassland increasingly turned to desert. Even as this process worked its impoverishing effects, human lifestyles changed. Sometime around 8000 B.C., Stone Age hunters were succeeded by herders, who grazed cattle, sheep and goats wherever the pasturage was best, and by farmers, who scratched a living from the soil. Theirs was a steadily diminishing realm. The drying that occurred in the wake of the Ice Age eventually left two thirds of the peninsula only marginally inhabitable. Nevertheless, nomadic herders continued to roam through the interior, making the most of oasis pasturage and water.

By 3000 B.C., when the first advanced civilizations were emerging in the East, the Arabians who lived in the coastal settlements were engaged in a maritime trade with the Sumerians to the north-east of themselves and the Indians to the south-east. Copper mined in Oman is found in the Sumerian ruins of Mesopotamia, as are pearls that had been fished out of the Arabian Gulf; and statues from the Indus valley and Sumerian pottery have been unearthed in Oman and Bahrain. Sumerian clay tablets record that the ships that entered the Tigris and the Euphrates Rivers from the Arabian Gulf were built in Dilmun—the ancient name of modern Bahrain.

Neither the Sumerians nor the Arabians themselves described the ships, but some clue as to their construction can be gleaned from Marco Polo, even

A pruner clambers up a date palm near Nizwa, Oman. Almost 100 varieties of dates are grown on the Arabian Peninsula, many in irrigated groves like this one. To ensure a bountiful crop, the trees are pollinated by hand.

though he did not sail into Eastern seas until a few millennia later. "Their ships are wretched affairs," he wrote with chauvinistic disdain, "for they have no iron fastenings and are only stitched together with twine made from the husk of the Indian nut"–by which he meant coconut. "Hence it is a perilous business to go on a voyage in one of those ships, and many of them are lost." Nearly 800 years have passed since Marco Polo wrote those words, yet even today similar vessels ply the shallow waters of the Arabian Gulf.

The earliest picture of an Arab ship was drawn in Mesopotamia in the 13th century A.D. and would have been more or less contemporaneous with the ships that Marco Polo saw. It shows a raked stem and a steering board attached to the sternpost. The captain sits on the poop deck, a handful of loin-clothed crewmen tend the rigging and six beturbaned gentlemen–who are presumably merchants–peer out from portholes. Early accounts suggest that several merchants travelled together aboard ship, each with his own goods to sell; and at least one such account suggests that each had a separate cabin–not for his own comfort, but to store the goods he intended to sell.

The tale of Sinbad the Sailor from *The Arabian Nights*, which was passed on by word of mouth for generations before it was finally set down in writing, suggests the nature of the merchants' peregrinations. "I bought me goods, merchandise and all needed for a voyage," Sinbad recounted, and "I embarked, with a company of merchants, on board a ship bound for Basra"–a port in what is today Iraq. "There we again embarked and sailed many days and nights, and we passed from isle to isle and sea to sea and shore to shore, buying and selling and bartering everywhere the ship touched."

The sea routes that the Arabians followed can only be conjectured. They may well have taken a coastal route; by hugging every shore they could stop for water and provisions and barter where there was a settlement.

Starting from a point on the west shore of the Arabian Gulf, a passage north would eventually take a vessel to Mesopotamia; from there it could go down the opposite side of the Gulf along the coast of Persia (modern Iran) and so to India. Alternatively, by sailing south along the west shore of the Gulf and through the Strait of Hormuz a vessel could set a course for three ports on Arabia's south coast–Muscat in the Gulf of Oman, Qana at the foot of the Hadramaut uplands and Aden at the base of the Yemeni mountains.

From each of those ports, by the start of the first millennium B.C., if not before, a route went overland to meet an inland caravan route that skirted the worst of the desert and followed wadis, the dried beds of the ancient rivers that had long since ceased to flow. The wadis not only cut through the mountains and uplands, but they also served to lead travellers to the desert's oases, where wells provided water and date palms provided nourishing food and the blessed relief of shade. Among them the roads formed a continuous network that bound the far-flung oases of the peninsula together.

Southern Arabia had one major advantage over other regions: it was rich in agriculture. This part of the peninsula was watered by rains coming from the mountains, and here arose the spectacular kingdoms that dazzled the ancient world. They possessed "a great quantity of articles wrought in gold and silver, as couches, tripods, basins, drinking vessels, to which we must add the costly magnificence of their houses, for the doors, walls and roofs are variegated with inlaid ivory, gold, silver and precious stones," wrote the Greek historian Strabo in the first century B.C.

Strabo was describing two different peoples—the Sabaeans, a stratified society of kings, priests, merchants and artisans who made up the kingdom of Saba, in the region of today's North Yemen, and the Gerrhaeans, a people who controlled the business of the Arabian Gulf port of Gerrha, which is thought to have been in the area south of modern Dhahran. But Strabo might have been writing of any of several Arabian kingdoms, because part of the peninsula—from the area of North Yemen, east to

Oman and north along the Arabian Gulf to Bahrain—is rich in the ruins of an urban civilization.

Among their creations were a palace with a roof of a single slab of alabaster said to be so translucent it was possible to distinguish between a crow and a kite flying above: alabaster statues adorned with lapis lazuli and gold: and police ordinances inscribed on pillars at the entrances to their cities. "They bartered spices for gold and silver and precious stones," Strabo wrote of the Sabaeans, "and had no need of things imported from the outside."

Strabo was biased; the very gold, silver and precious stones he cited came from Africa and India—but the Sabaeans had no need for Rome's particular exports, which were wheat and wine, because the lush green slopes of Saba yielded grains and delectable fruits. They did so because the Sabaeans had a system of irrigation unparalleled in the ancient world—a fact that was all the more remarkable in that they had no permanent rivers to exploit and had to figure out a way to conserve and control the run-off from a rainfall of only 90 centimetres a year.

Their solution was an elaborate system of dams. The most spectacular was the Ma'rib Dam, a 610-metre-wide construction that deflected water flowing down from the mountains, some of which are as high as 3,650 metres, and distributed it over 1,600 hectares.

In addition to dams, the Sabaeans built rectangular reservoirs, 75 metres long and 1.5 metres deep, for conserving rainfall above ground. They also made ingenious use of underground springs. They learnt not only how to dig as deep as 50 metres to tap the water where it flowed, but also to direct it by means of a network of subterra-

nean canals to distant fields. Finally, they terraced their mountain slopes so that they could make use of every bit of soil. To this very day the Yemenis terrace their slopes in the same way (pages 30-31). Then as now, the result was a rich yield of grain, dates, almonds, pomegranates, melons and aromatics.

Of all the crops the ancient Arabians harvested, none could match the importance of frankincense and myrrh, the gum resins of two trees that grew in wild profusion on the inland-facing slopes of the mountains on the peninsula's southern coast.

Frankincense and myrrh, which are little more than fragrant curiosities in the modern world, had wide and important uses in ancient times—in religion, in medicine, in public sanitation and in personal grooming. Alone, in combination with each other, or in compounds with other spices such as cinnamon, cassia and iris, frankincense and myrrh lent themselves to any number of ingenious preparations. Most commonly, frankincense was lit with glowing coals and then burnt in censers, the fragrant smoke wafting heavenward. But the aromatics could also be mixed with water or wine to make restorative tonics and soothing lotions, or with almond oil to yield sweet-smelling unguents.

As burnt offerings, they had a part in religious rituals and state ceremonials all over the ancient world. The souls of the dead and the prayers of priests were thought to ascend to heaven in the wispy smoke of incense, and so the Egyptians employed it in funerary rites and the priests at the Temple of Jerusalem burnt a kilogram of it when saying their daily prayers. The Greeks used incense to honour living heroes; they also used it to make an impression on

In this pre-Islamic rock carving, warriors armed with swords and spears raid a camel caravan. Such pictographs are found throughout the desert; most were the work of ancient caravaneers, whiling away the hours.

others. During an elaborate procession that Ptolemy II organized to flaunt his power in Alexandria in 278 B.C., a troop of women carrying censers 3 metres tall paraded past an admiring throng; behind them came another of boys in purple tunics bearing frankincense and myrrh on golden dishes, a formation of elephants and zebras drawing chariots, and a herd of camels laden with 135 kilograms of frankincense, 135 kilograms of myrrh and 90 kilograms of spices. The Romans used incense when cremating the dead; at the funeral of the dictator Sulla in 79 B.C., more than 210 litters were needed to carry all the aromatics to his pyre.

Besides their role in ceremonies, frankincense and myrrh had practical uses as well. In palace and temple halls, the sweet-smelling smoke dispelled the malodorous scent of unwashed bodies in the mass. Out-of-doors, it drove off the disease-bearing insects that swarmed about carrion and other refuse in the streets.

Frankincense and myrrh had perhaps their widest uses in pharmacology. The many potions that could be made from them were used to ease headache, the pains of childbirth, stiffness of joints, ulcers and abscesses; as antidotes to hemlock poisoning and insect bites; to stem haemorrhages and nosebleeds, coughing and nausea. Applied externally as poultices and balms, they soothed stinging eyes, earaches and chilblains.

Finally, people who could afford to do so used frankincense and myrrh to perfume themselves. Queen Hatshepsut of 15th-century B.C. Egypt is said to have scented her body with oil of myrrh, and the Song of Solomon rhapsodizes a lover whose "lips are lilies distilling pure myrrh".

In one guise or another these aromatics were used by the Sumerians, the Babylonians, the Egyptians, the Indians, the Minoans, the Assyrians, the Israelites, the Phoenicians, the Persians, the Parthians, the Greeks and the Romans—peoples who spanned nearly 4,000 years in time and 23 million square kilometres in area.

And all those peoples bought most of their myrrh and probably all of their frankincense from the Arabians, who had them in abundance. Myrrh and frankincense occur in some other tropi-

1

cal regions close by—in the islands off the peninsula; in Somalia, across the Gulf of Aden; and in parts of Ethiopia—but the most highly prized varieties grow only in the lime-rich soil of southern Arabia, in the 800-kilometre strip of territory known as the Dhufar in Oman and part of the Hadramaut in South Yemen. That limited range gave the aromatics special importance and the locale a certain mystery.

Outsiders seldom saw frankincense and myrrh in their original state. The earliest description of the trees was set down by the Greek botanist and geographer Theophrastus, who received his information from a Greek seaman sometime in the fourth century B.C. The frankincense tree "is not tall," Theophrastus wrote, "and it is much branched; it has a leaf like that of the pear, but much smaller and very grassy in colour. The myrrh tree is said to be still smaller in stature and more bushy; it is said to have a tough stem, which is contorted near the ground, and is stouter than a man's legs."

Both trees belong to the balsam family, whose bark is rich in resin. Both trees ooze their resin spontaneously— "weep their gum", in the description of a Greek seafarer—but the Arabians helped along the process by slashing the roots and the branches twice a year, once in summer and again in winter. "They make an incision where the bark appears to be fullest of juice and distended to its thinnest," recorded the Roman historian Pliny the Elder, "and the bark is loosened with a blow but not removed." As the gum oozed out of the tree, it hardened into tear-shaped lumps about the size of hens' eggs, sometimes bigger.

The collected lumps of frankincense and myrrh were stored away in moun-

tain caves and left six months or so to dry further. When they reached the crumbly stage, they were ready to be transported. From the caves the dried frankincense and myrrh were taken down to the shore and shipped by raft along the coast to Qana. Some ships from India and Africa were allowed, by fiat of the King of the Sabaeans, to trade their wares at Qana for frankincense, but most of the frankincense and myrrh was required to go inland to

Shabwa, the capital of the Hadramaut. There it was weighed, sorted, taxed and sold to the merchants who would carry it north to the Mediterranean and Mesopotamia together with the gold and silver, silks and gems that came by sea from India to Qana.

To make the journey north, merchants banded together in great convoys; a caravan might have as many as 2,500 camels and 300 merchants, guides, guards and drivers. For each

26

Two Omanis scrape the bark of a frankincense tree to start the aromatic resin flowing. Frankincense is still used as an air and water sweetener and as medicine in parts of the Arabian Peninsula, Africa and India.

merchant, the journey was a costly investment. Beginning at Shabwa, fixed portions of the cargo had to be given to royal retainers, according to Pliny, "but besides these the guards and the gate-keepers and servants also have their pickings; indeed all along the route they keep on paying, at one place for water, at another for fodder, or the charges for lodging at the halts, and then again payment is made to the customs officers of our empire."

Kings and tribal chieftains all along the way took great precautions to see that they got their share of the trade. At Timna, the next city after Shabwa, a small obelisk about 1.5 metres high stood in the marketplace with a listing of the market regulations; one of them indicated the taxes due to the king. On the next leg of the route, the approach to the city of Ma'rib to this day contains the remains of a paved road that is some 450 metres long and lined on either side with stone walls that converge from 18 metres at the start to about 8 metres at the end. Archaeologists speculate that the purpose of this curious construction was to funnel the caravans through in single file so that they could be counted and taxed.

As the caravans proceeded north from Najran, the frontier of the lush incense country, they went through the mountains that run the length of the Red Sea coast, or they turned east across the central escarpment that leads to modern Riyadh and thence to the Arabian Gulf coast *en route* to Mesopotamia. Either way, the land became increasingly barren. And were it not for the camel, the Arabians would have had no means of transporting their frankincense and myrrh—much less the lucrative products of India—to the markets in the north.

In the camel they had a beast that could negotiate the harsh expanses of their land as no other creature could. The camel could carry a load upwards of 180 kilograms. Its padded feet could tread over unstable soil and scorching sand. Its stomach could digest the desert's toughest thornbushes. At a single feeding it could drink up to 150 litres of water too salty for human consumption, and then go for up to 10 days without further watering because its body conserved moisture (*page 71*). In addition to all that, it yielded milk for its drivers to drink, hair that could be woven into cloth and rope, and skin that could be fashioned into saddle-bags, sandals and water buckets that enabled the humans to make the trip. And its dried dung was a ready source of cooking fuel in a treeless land.

A glance at a map shows how long the caravan route was. The distance from Timna, at the southern end of the peninsula, to Gaza, its outlet on the Mediterranean, is about 2,400 kilometres and Pliny wrote that the journey between those termini was done in 65 stages. That means the journey took at least 65 days, and it may have taken more if a stage required a stopover to negotiate for the next leg of the trip.

Negotiating for passage was part of every caravan journey, and it could be complicated. Of necessity, the stops were made at the oases, where water and pasturage were already claimed by the local nomads. The caravaneers had to pay for the use of the wells and the pastures; they did so by choosing from their cargoes such gifts as cloth, copper bowls, and—if the chief was important enough—gold and silver cups and bowls. The nomads might also claim the right to provide the camels, the drivers, the scouts and the guides to lead the caravan through their own territory and safely on to the next. If this was the case, yet another presentation of gifts was called for.

The whole procedure was surrounded by complex ritual–the elaborate courtesies that were exchanged during Ibn Saud's expedition in 1939 reflects the vestigial observance of the custom–and in ancient times any breach in the etiquette meant risking the wrath of the desert nomads, who took revenge by raiding the caravans. By the time all the formalities had been gone through, the 65 stages may well have stretched over many months.

The complex logistics of the transactions led to the growth along the way of caravan cities–places that acquired wealth of their own, not so much through settled occupations such as agriculture and craftsmanship (though some agriculture to ensure food and some crafts such as tentmaking and weaving were practised) as through the profits that were to be had in managing the caravan traffic.

Some cities began as colonies of the Sabaean kingdom and were probably settled by Sabaeans with an interest in expediting the northbound passage of frankincense and myrrh and other cargoes. The celebrated Queen of Sheba, who by biblical account visited King Solomon in Judea with "camels laden with spices, great quantities of gold and precious stones", is thought by some scholars to have been the leading personage of such a settlement. Other towns grew up when a strong tribal leader was lured in from the desert and made it his business to oversee the orderly flow of traffic and to ensure that the profits were to his kin. Such a place was Mecca, which began as a watering hole in ancient times and by the heyday

1

of the Arabians' caravan trade was a major stop on the route to the north.

That lucrative trade continued into the early years of the Christian era. In the third century A.D. it went into eclipse. The reasons are complex and shrouded in the mysteries of unrecorded history. But two facts stand out. One is that the Romans, who expanded their empire by land across Syria and into Mesopotamia, took up trading by sea. The other is that as Christianity gained a foothold throughout the world, it began to change tastes and customs everywhere.

By the year 48 B.C., the Roman Emperor Julius Caesar had seized the once-mighty Egyptian Empire. Not the least of the assets he won was access to the Red Sea—a body of water that ancient mariners ventured into at their peril. "The country inland is peopled by rascally men, who live in villages and nomadic camps, by whom those sailing off the middle course are plundered, and those surviving shipwrecks are taken for slaves," states the *Periplus of the Erythrean Sea*, a first-century A.D. account written by an anonymous Greek mariner. Quite apart from the Arabian pirates, the sea itself was a menace. "Navigation is dangerous along this whole coast of Arabia, which is without harbours, with bad anchorages, foul, inaccessible because of breakers and rocks, and terrible in every way," the *Periplus* goes on.

Nevertheless, the Romans could manage the perils of the Red Sea because they had the technology to turn out the biggest and sturdiest vessels yet seen in the ancient world. Roman merchantmen were up to 55 metres long and as much as 18 metres in the beam, and had two or three decks. They had keels of oak and planking of fir, cedar

and pine; they were superbly crafted with snug-fitting mortises and tenons and were sheathed in lead. Such sturdy craft sped easily through the Red Sea. And the Romans dealt with the pirates by stationing archers on deck. Thus fortified, they sailed south through the Red Sea, out into the Gulf of Aden and then on to the Arabian Sea—which up to that time had been the exclusive province of the Arabians, the Africans and the Indians.

Just when the Romans first sailed into the area with their ships is not re-

corded. But about 90 B.C. a seaman named Hippalus undertook such a journey. Although no one knows who he was, he made the important discovery that he could use the south-west monsoons of summer—as the Arabians did—to beat a path diagonally across the north-eastern reaches of the Indian Ocean and then return on the northeast wind of winter, thereby eliminating the twisting route along the coasts of Arabia and Iran. When Hippalus appeared in Rome with pepper, cinnamon, ginger and Indian silks that had

The ruins of ancient Baraqish rise from the desert in North Yemen. As its sturdy walls attest, Baraqish was a major city of the Minaean kingdom, which flourished in southern Arabia between 400 and 100 B.C.

not had to pass through Arabian customs, the Arabian monopoly on trading with the East was doomed.

For the Arabians, there was worse to come. In 325 A.D., the Emperor Constantine declared Christianity the official religion of the Roman Empire. Not long afterwards he issued a proclamation that banned many of the cherished customs of the pagan world–among them the practice of cremating the dead. The banning of cremation resulted in a severe reduction in the market for frankincense. The resin continued to be used in other rituals, but in far smaller quantities.

With the loss of the incense trade, the southern cities lost their major source of income; and with the Romans carrying goods by sea, the caravan trade fell off in the string of cities that bound the peninsula from south to north. Citizens of the southern cities, the first to be impoverished, moved north to the caravan cities in search of livelihood. In time citizens of the north abandoned the caravan cities and moved back out to the desert, where they resumed their nomadic quest for pasturage–living more or less peaceably when the oases were bountiful, raiding one another's encampments when they were not.

Not much is known about the Arabians for the next 300 years, for the nomads kept no written records. In the south, palaces fell into disrepair, terraced fields grew up in weeds and sometime late in the sixth century the great dam at Ma'rib burst. In later years that catastrophe found its way into the Muslim scriptures, where it was explained as the result of divine disfavour; but whatever the interpretation, the event underscores the disintegration of southern Arabia.

Through it all, however, local trading continued. Even in their wanderings, the northern Arabs bartered with one another, swapping milk, sheep, goats and camels for dates, grain and coffee, and in doing so kept alive a few of the erstwhile caravan cities. In fact, for three months of every year they suspended raiding and came together to trade, to stage story-telling contests that exalted the prowess of the biggest and most valorous of the tribes–and to pray to their tribal gods.

By the seventh century A.D., the old caravan city of Mecca had emerged as the most important of the surviving cities; and its ruling tribe, the Quraysh, had emerged pre-eminent among the desert people. Into that tribe in about 570 a son named Muhammad was born, who would preach a gospel compounded of ancient tribal beliefs, Judaism and the new Christianity. Out of his preaching was to come the faith of Islam–one of the world's major systems of spiritual belief. Islam would give the Arabs a new sense of collective identity and set the stage for their second act upon the international stage.

A FORGOTTEN WORLD

Tucked away in the mountainous south-west of the Arabian Peninsula is a land where 8.5 million people live much as Arabians did when the Romans wrote of *Arabia Felix*–Arabia the Blessed. This is the Yemen Arab Republic, called North Yemen to distinguish it from the People's Republic of Yemen, its south-eastern neighbour.

North Yemen has a 50 to 75-centimetre annual rainfall that washes down its 3,600-metre mountains to the valleys and plateaux below, yielding a cornucopia of the dates, oranges and other exotica that aroused Roman envy. The same mountains seal the people off from the desert beyond. In their isolation, they have preserved ancient customs, from the way they plough their fields to the decorations that brighten their homes. But change is not far away, the discovery of oil in north-east North Yemen in 1984 may soon alter the land and lifestyle of the people.

In Mawsat, a village in the region of Jabal Barat, sheep rest in front of a mud-brick house whose windows and door are trimmed with distinctive bands of colour, a Yemeni tradition that dates back to ancient times.

The terraced slopes of Jabal Milhan rise out of the mist to an altitude of 2,500 metres. From these terraces– fertilized with manure and ashes from cooking fires–come vegetables and fruit for surrounding cities.

Two young girls bring goats in their care to water at a cistern in the Uthmah region: herded collectively during the day, the goats are taken back to their owners in the evening.

In the remote mountain village of Shahara, two women trudge uphill to a cistern, one of 12 that collect rain—the only source of water. The village women make such trips twice daily.

At the end of a stormy afternoon on the arid northern Tihama plain, village women come to draw water. The well is open to all, but each woman brings her own cord and pulley.

A *qat* seller from Jabal Sabir–where all of that lucrative trade is handled by women–can afford to wear gold jewellery; Yemenis spend as much as a third of family income on *qat*.

Ploughing crosswise to old furrows to avoid soil erosion, farmers prepare terraces for planting. The country's most profitable cash crop is *qat*, a green leaf that yields a mildly narcotic effect when it is chewed.

Water pipes and bundles of fresh *qat* leaves fill a *mafraj*, a room where Yemeni men hold daily *qat*-chewing sessions. This party celebrated a wedding and cost more than $2,000.

Dressed in Western-style jackets over their traditional skirts, two men at the market in San'a chat at the front of a stand that sells the kind of curved daggers worn by most Yemeni men. Such daggers are frequently handed down from father to son.

At *sug Sebt*–Saturday's market–villagers crowd the narrow paths between stone huts that serve as shops. The merchants at the weekly market sell everything from meat, grain and fruit to cosmetics, medicinal herbs and cans of tuna fish–not to mention the ubiquitous *qat*.

A muezzin, or crier, calls the faithful to prayer from the minaret of a mosque in Tuhayta, North Yemen. Muslims pray five times a day–at daybreak, at noon, in the afternoon, at sunset and in the evening–no matter where in the world they may be at the time.

THE SPIRITUAL CORE

Long before Mecca became a focus of Muslim devotion, it was an important city. Lying about half-way up the trade route that ran along the Red Sea coast from the southern reaches of *Arabia Felix* to the Mediterranean, it attracted caravans carrying frankincense, myrrh and other luxuries of the ancient world. The road forked here. One of its branches headed east to the Arabian Gulf and points beyond; and hardly a day's march to the west lay Jidda, a port of entry for ships coming from Egypt and Abyssinia.

But for all its convenience as a trading centre, Mecca takes its name from a Sabaean word meaning "sanctuary". The infinitely varied mix of merchants who gathered there to buy and sell and to get fresh relays of camels also used the stop to worship their diverse gods.

In the Arabia of the seventh century A.D., the majority of Mecca's visitors believed in a host of deities who played specialized roles in their lives. To the Meccans themselves, the most important of the gods was Allah, patron of the Quraysh, a tribe that had provided the city's leading merchants and rulers for more than a century. But some of the Meccans held quite different beliefs. Judaism, with its uncompromising monotheism, was nearly 2,000 years old, and several Jewish merchants, doctors and musicians had come from Palestine to settle in Mecca. Christianity was in its seventh century and was represented there by colonists from Abyssinia, Byzantium and Syria.

Besides the divinities, there were a number of spirits—some benevolent,

others evil—to respect or fear. They included angels, who carried out missions of the gods, and demons called jinns, who worked evil upon individuals. Good or bad, such spirits were believed to inhabit rocks, trees, wells and caves, which themselves were feared or revered for awesome events associated with them.

Mecca's most hallowed rock, the so-called Black Stone, was a meteorite said by legend to have been sent from heaven by Allah to Abraham, the Semitic patriarch whom Arabians, Jews and Christians alike looked upon as their common ancestor. At some unknown period in history the stone had been enclosed in a cube-shaped shrine known as the Ka'aba, which in time came to have the importance of a temple. Inside the temple were altars to more than 300 deities, reflecting the plethora of tribes and peoples who came and went through Mecca.

Through the centuries the custom had grown up of gathering at Mecca at least once a year—probably around the time of the autumnal equinox, when the worst of the peninsula's heat began to subside. The pilgrims made ritual circumambulations of the Ka'aba. They drank at the Zamzam well, where Abraham's concubine Hagar and their son Ishmael had found water after the patriarch had abandoned them to the desert. The pilgrims also visited nearby Mount Arafat, which was the site of another shrine, and they ceremoniously cast stones at the pillars to drive out evil spirits. When everything else had been done, they sacrificed camels and

sheep as burnt offerings intended to please their gods.

Although ostensibly the pilgrimages existed for the purpose of honouring the gods, dispelling the evil spirits and praying for a good year to come, they also brought together kinfolk who had been scattered by nomadism and trading ventures. Thus the pilgrimages became occasions for celebration as well as for worship.

The pilgrims joined with local city people to stage story-telling contests that served as vehicles for perfecting poetry in the Arabic language, one of the most musical of spoken tongues in the entire world. They also served to transmit the common history of the nomadic and settled tribes. (It was through these story-telling contests that such figures as Adam and Eve, Noah, Abraham and Moses became known to the people throughout the desert region and in the settled areas on its fringes.) Finally, the story-telling helped to exalt the prowess of the biggest, strongest and most valorous of the tribes—and indirectly it also perpetuated tribal grudges and tribal feuds.

The pilgrimages were regarded as excuses for making money, and the Quraysh, the strongmen of the region, used these occasions to exploit the less fortunate tribes. They took tribute from the pilgrims—even though many of them were too poor to pay.

Within and without the context of the pilgrimages, law in Mecca was a haphazard thing. The powerful men of the Quraysh did as they chose. Citizens who felt they had been dealt with unfairly had no means of redress, only the hope that magic would work in their favour; questions of "justice" were resolved by the casting of arrows kept alongside the statue of the moon-god in the temple. Where an arrow fell, the position in which it lay and whether or not it broke might determine who was guilty and who was innocent of wrongdoing, and whether or not to embark on a feud. Once a feud began, it was apt to continue for many years. One feud that had arisen out of the theft of a single she-camel towards the end of the fifth century dragged on for four decades.

The status quo of Meccan society changed abruptly in the seventh century with the advent of Muhammad. Out of the polytheistic confusion and social inequities of the era, he founded one of the world's great religions. At the same time he gave the nomadic tribes of the Arabian Peninsula their first sense of unity and secured for his homeland a permanent place in the history of the world.

The details of Muhammad's birth and early life are indefinite and known only through the legends that have grown up around him. According to some of the most popular ones, he was born about the year 570, into the Quraysh tribe, more specifically into the Hashimite clan. (A number of branches of the clan survive to this day; perhaps the most famous representative is King Hussein of Jordan.)

Among the Quraysh tribe of Muhammad's day, some clans were more prosperous than others. Several of Muhammad's relatives held important posts. His paternal grandfather sent trading caravans to Yemen and Syria and supplied food and water to the pilgrims who came to Mecca. One of his uncles, al-Abbas, was keeper of the

Zamzam well, and another, Abu Talib, was collector of a tax to help the poor.

But Muhammad's immediate family—according to the legends—was not especially well off. His father died before he was born and left his mother a modest legacy of one slave, five camels and a few sheep—barely enough to keep her in milk and wool. She was forced to send Muhammad to live with a nomadic tribe in the desert. When the boy was six years old, she could afford to take him back, but he had hardly returned to her when she died. He was then sent to his grandfather—only to have the grandfather die, too. He ended up living with his uncle Abu Talib, who raised him and took him on caravan journeys to Syria when Muhammad was about 12 years old.

Thus, before he reached adolescence, Muhammad had already had a number of experiences that in the years to come would profoundly influence his thinking and his character. He had

been exposed to the two prevailing social groups of the peninsula—the merchants of the caravan trade and the nomads of the desert. He had had members of his family removed from him by death. He knew what it was to be at the mercy of relatives richer than himself. He had been introduced to foreign ways in Syria, a major cultural centre of the Middle Eastern world.

Muhammad grew into a man of unremarkable appearance. A contemporary described him as "of middle height," and having "hair that was neither straight nor curly, with a large head, large eyes, heavy eyelashes, a reddish tint in the eyes, thick-bearded, broad-shouldered, with thick hands and feet." By the time he reached 25, however, he had earned a reputation in Mecca as a capable and honest businessman and had come to the attention of a well-to-do widow in her forties. Her name was Khadija, and she had inherited a caravan business from one of her two late husbands. She apparently sent a matchmaker to ask Muhammad to marry her and take on her caravan interests, and he did.

During his marriage to Khadija, Muhammad fathered two or three sons, who died in infancy, and four daughters, who would survive. The trading he conducted on his wife's behalf gave him material comforts—and evidently plenty of time to think. He seems to have spent long, solitary vigils meditating in a cave on Mount Hira, on the outskirts of Mecca. It was during one such retreat in the year 610, when he was about 40 years old, that he had the experience that was to transform him from a run-of-the-mill trader into one of the giants of history.

According to his own personal account of the event, Muhammad heard

This 16th-century Turkish miniature shows the archangel Gabriel revealing a passage of the Koran to Muhammad. The Prophet's face is covered, in keeping with the Muslim tradition of never portraying his features.

the archangel Gabriel speak to him, telling him that he was the "Messenger of Allah". Muhammad added that the archangel pressed him "so tightly that I thought it was death".

Not surprisingly, Muhammad was frightened by the incident and thought that he had been possessed by a demon. He told Khadija, who relayed his account to a Christian kinsman. This man came to the conclusion that Muhammad had been granted the same kind of divine inspiration that had been given to Moses, and that Muhammad himself would become a leader of his own people.

As time went on, Muhammad continued to have revelations. "There is no god but Him, the Living, the Eternal One," Muhammad heard. "His throne is as vast as the heavens and the earth, and the preservation of both does not weary Him. He is the Exalted, the Immense One." Muhammad reached the conclusion that the polytheism of his contemporaries was all wrong; there was no god but Allah, and He was the creator of heaven and earth.

For the time being, Muhammad kept his reflections to himself and a few intimates–Khadija, his cousin Ali, who was the son of his uncle Abu Talib, and a man by the name of Abu Bakr, his closest friend. But in 613 he had a revelation in which he perceived that he was being ordered to "rise and warn" the people. He now began preaching publicly in Mecca.

Rebuking his listeners for serving "idols which can neither help nor harm themselves, and which have no power over life or death," Muhammad relayed these words from Allah: "It was Allah who made the heavens and the earth. He sends down water from the sky with which He brings forth fruits

Astride a mythical steed, Muhammad ascends to seventh heaven, where elysian pleasures await him. Muslims believe that Gabriel took the Prophet on a seven-stage celestial tour, introducing him to Adam, Moses, Jesus and other biblical figures.

AN ABIDING PASSION FOR THE SPOKEN WORD

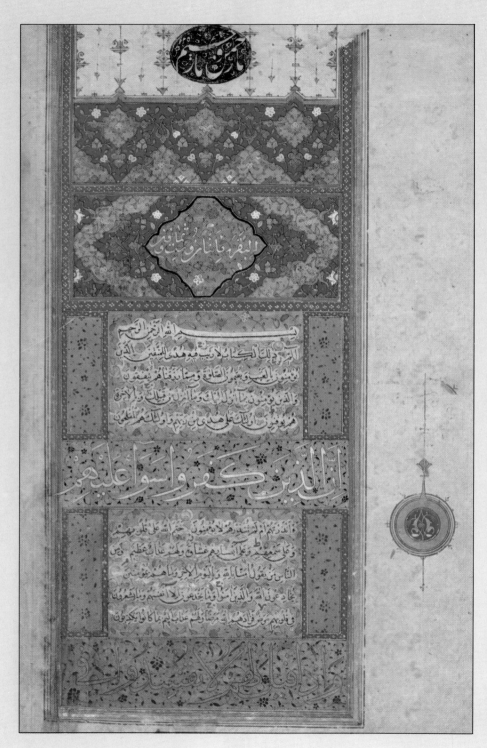

When the archangel Gabriel revealed the Koran to Muhammad in the seventh century, say Muslims, his first utterance was "Recite!" Muhammad and his followers obeyed, memorizing the Islamic message and spreading it by the spoken word. Even after the Koran had been written down, oral transmission was essential; the scripture was in a form of Arabic without vowel marks, so words could be misread unless pronunciations were known. Special schools taught succeeding generations to recite the holy book correctly.

But the Arab oral tradition pre-dates the Koran. Long before Muhammad's time, nomads chose words, which could fill the long hours on camelback and around campfires, as their primary mode of artistic expression. "The beauty of man," says a Bedouin maxim, "lies in the eloquence of his tongue."

The most admired tongues were those of poets. Tribesmen said that only three occasions merited congratulations—the birth of a son, the foaling of a mare and the emergence of a new bard. Arab poets work in a language so rich and complex that their verses defy satisfactory translation. But lines like the following—by a young sixth-century Bedouin poetically thumbing his nose at critics of his drinking and wenching— transcend any language barrier:
I'm a generous fellow, one that soaks himself in his lifetime;
You'll know tomorrow, when we're dead, which of us is the thirsty one.
Today's Bedouin are still in love with words, and they often break into spontaneous poetry at no greater provocation than discovering a good grazing patch.

When this ornate Koran cover was made in the 16th century, 900 years after Muhammad's death, more Muslims still learnt the scripture by word of mouth than by reading it.

for your sustenance. He drives the ships which by His leave sail the ocean in your service. He has created rivers for your benefit, and the sun and the moon, which steadfastly pursue their courses. And He has subdued to you the night and the day. He grants you all that you ask Him. If you reckoned Allah's favours you could not count them. Truly, man is wicked and thankless."

Muhammad went on to preach that humanity must submit to Allah's will. Included in Allah's will was the injunction that the rich must share their wealth—a gift from Allah—with the poor. Giving urgency to the message, Muhammad warned there would be a Day of Judgment, when all men and women would be held accountable for the lives they had lived. Those who had honoured God's commands could expect a new life of ease in paradise; those who disobeyed would merit the terrible punishment of hellfire. Muhammad called this new religion Islam, meaning "submission to God", and he named his followers Muslims, meaning "those who submit".

As he preached, he attracted a growing number of followers to the new religion. In time, some of his adherents began to set down on palm leaves and on clay tablets the pronouncements that Muhammad delivered as Allah's messenger. Those inscriptions were later to be gathered to form the *Koran*, a book of 114 *suras*, or verses, that rank among the most eloquent of scriptures in all of religious history.

To Meccans who were bewildered by the plethora of capricious and often contradictory gods, and particularly to those who were excluded from the material well-being and the power of the wealthy merchants, Muhammad's preaching gave a comforting sense of order and of hope.

But to many of the elders and the merchants of the Quraysh tribe—including some of his own uncles—the message was highly unsettling. Muhammad was urging the adoration of a single god, and their revenues depended on the pilgrims' coming to worship as many gods as there were tribes. Should those pilgrims be discouraged from coming to Mecca, the Quraysh elders would stand to lose a major source of their wealth.

But Muhammad was not merely elevating one god above the others. He was delivering a social message: that the strong were oppressing the weak, when instead they should be aiding the unfortunates among them. The Quraysh could not listen with equanimity to such charges against themselves, particularly when the charges came from someone who was speaking as a messenger of God. They met Muhammad's sermons with derision. They disrupted his meetings, and they stoned and beat some of his followers. One Quraysh clan, the Umayyads, turned against Muhammad's fellow Hashimites and boycotted them. For three years no Hashimite was able to buy or sell anything in Mecca.

Muhammad soon had sufferings of another and more personal sort to endure. Khadija died in 617, and shortly afterwards so did his uncle Abu Talib, who had been one of his most loyal supporters. Then, suddenly, in 622 Muhammad's luck began to turn for the better. A group of pilgrims who had come for the annual gathering at Mecca heard him preach, liked what they heard and offered him refuge among them in the town of Yathrib, 435 kilometres to the north. That town had a number of feuding Arabian tribes whose disputes might profit from an arbiter such as Muhammad. It also had a large settlement of Jewish merchants and craftsmen, whose own beliefs were not dissimilar to Muhammad's. Furthermore, he quite possibly had relatives in the pilgrims' city; Yathrib was where his mother had been born.

For whatever reason, Muhammad accepted the invitation, and a large contingent of Meccans emigrated with him to Yathrib in the year 622. That event, known as the *hijra*, or "flight", was later to become sacred to Muslims, and the date came to mark the official beginning of the Islamic community and therefore of Islamic history. The name of Yathrib was changed to Madinat al-Nabi, "City of the Prophet", known in English as Medina.

In Medina, Muhammad lived simply, in a house he built himself. It consisted of a courtyard enclosed by a mud-brick wall. Against the east wall were huts for his wives; he married several after the death of Khadija. The courtyard was shaded with palm trees. It proved to be the first mosque; Muhammad preached his sermons there, leaning against the trunk of a palm tree, speaking slowly and carefully and casting his eyes heavenward, as if reading a text from on high.

As his hosts had hoped, the quarrelsome tribes of Medina were soon able to look beyond their narrow tribal concerns and to put aside their personal grievances. Listening to Muhammad, they gradually submitted to the commands he issued in the name of Allah. They found in Muhammad a leader they could share in common—just as within the tribes, families looked to their strongest and wisest members as the sheikh. In Medina, Muhammad had founded a community that did not

A CHRONOLOGY OF KEY EVENTS

c.5000 B.C. Agricultural settlements spring up on the Arabian Gulf coast of the Arabian Peninsula.

4000-2000 B.C. The Dilmun civilization dominates Arabia's east coast to Bahrain and serves as the trading link with Mesopotamia and the Indus valley.

1500-1200 B.C. The camel is domesticated by desert tribes.

1000 B.C. The Sabaean kingdom, possible home of the Queen of Sheba (*below*), is established in the south-west corner of the Arabian Peninsula.

350 B.C.-100 A.D. Arabians called Nabataeans control trade routes in Jordan and northern Arabia.

70 A.D. Destruction of the Temple in Jerusalem brings great numbers of Jews to Yemen.

106 A Roman legion destroys the Nabataean capital of Petra.

100-200 The Al Azd tribe, ancestors of present-day Omani rulers, migrates to Oman.

226 The Persian Empire stimulates sea trade with many settlements along the Arabian Gulf.

356 Christian missionaries enter the Arabian Peninsula.

c.550 The great dam of Ma'rib, heart of Yemen's irrigation system, bursts and ends an era of prosperity.

570 The Abyssinians establish a protectorate over southern Arabia.

c.570 The Prophet Muhammad is born in Mecca.

575 The Abyssinians are ousted from Arabia by the Persians.

613 Muhammad begins to preach openly in the city of Mecca, but his message is rejected.

622 Muhammad moves with his followers to Medina. The Muslim calendar dates from this migration, known throughout Islam as the *hijra*.

630 Muhammad returns to Mecca with an army of followers, smashing idols but preserving the sacred Black Stone housed in the Ka'aba (*below*).

632 Muhammad dies.

632-634 Abu Bakr, Muhammad's father-in-law, succeeds the Prophet as leader of Islam and makes further geographic gains for the faith.

634-644 Umar succeeds Abu Bakr as leader; Islamic forces under his rule advance through the Persian and Byzantine Empires.

642 Egypt falls to the Arabian army. The expansion of Islam into North Africa follows.

644 Uthman succeeds Umar as leader; at his instigation the Koran is compiled from existing manuscripts.

656 Muhammad's son-in-law Ali succeeds to the leadership of Islam.

661 Ali is assassinated; Islam splits into rival factions, known as the Shiite and the Sunni.

661-750 Islam extends from Spain to Mongolia. Administrative power shifts from Arabia to Damascus.

750-1258 Baghdad functions as the temporal centre of Islam, effectively bringing to an end Arabian control of the Muslim empire.

c.1225 The port of Hormuz becomes the focus of Arabian Gulf trade.

1507 The Portuguese enter the Gulf and secure Hormuz.

1517 Ottoman Turks conquer Egypt and bring Yemen under their control.

1550 The Turks seize control of the Hijaz, northern Arabia, and the Gulf coast as far south as Qatar.

1618 The British East India Company establishes a trading centre at Mocha, on the south-west coast of Yemen.

1622 The Persians and the British forces unite to drive the Portuguese from Hormuz.

1680 The Dutch set up trading posts and achieve mercantile supremacy in the northern Gulf.

1695 Omani pirates prey on British and Dutch shipping in the Gulf.

1703 Muhammad ibn Abd al-Wahhab, founder of the fundamentalist Wahhabi movement, is born.

1742 Abd al-Wahhab is welcomed by Muhammad ibn Saud, an ancestor of Abd al-Aziz ibn Saud, first King of Saudi Arabia, after being expelled from his home town for religious fanaticism.

1761 The sheikhdom of Abu Dhabi is founded on the Gulf coast.

1765 The British become the primary European influence when the Dutch abandon their settlements in the Gulf.

1773 Al Saud warriors in alliance with Al Wahhabi religious leaders capture the city of Riyadh.

1803 The Wahhabi influence spreads as far as Yemen.

1820 Seven coastal sheikhs sign the General Treaty of Peace with Britain to suppress piracy and the slave trade.

1839 The British take Aden, "the eye of Yemen", by force.

1861 Bahrain and Great Britain sign the Perpetual Treaty of Peace and Friendship.

1902 With fewer than 50 men, Abd al-Aziz ibn Saud conquers Riyadh.

1913 Abd al-Aziz becomes sovereign of the Najd and al-Hasa.

1916 Qatar signs a protective treaty with Britain. Abd al-Aziz assumes control of the ultrapuritanical Ikhwan (Wahhabi) movement, using it to gain the loyalty of tribal sheikhs.

1926 Abd al-Aziz conquers Mecca, Jidda and Medina.

1932 The Kingdom of Saudi Arabia is proclaimed. Oil production begins in southern Bahrain.

1933 King Abd al-Aziz grants an oil concession that leads to the development of the first well *(below)*.

1937 The port of Aden becomes a British crown colony.

1938 Oil is discovered in Kuwait. Saudi Arabia begins oil production. Said bin Taimur becomes the Sultan of Oman and isolates the country.

1945 Saudi Arabia, Egypt and Yemen create the Arab League.

1953 King Abd al-Aziz ibn Saud dies and is succeeded by his son Saud ibn Abd al-Aziz Al Saud.

1961. Kuwait gains independence.

1962 The Army overthrows the imam, setting up a republic in North Yemen.

1964 King Saud is deposed; he is succeeded by his younger brother Faisal ibn Abdal-Aziz Al Saud. Slavery is abolished.

1967 The People's Democratic Republic of Yemen (South Yemen) is founded.

1970 A bloodless coup in Oman ousts Sultan Said, installs his son Qaboos bin Said as ruler. National Day fireworks *(below)* commemorate Qaboos' many

development programmes.

1971 Bahrain and Qatar become independent. United Arab Emirates is formed. South Yemen institutes sweeping nationalization laws.

1973 OPEC influences oil pricing for the first time.

1974 Army officers seize control of North Yemen. Fighting between the two Yemens takes place sporadically until 1979.

1975 King Faisal *(below)* is assassinated; he is succeeded by his brother Khalid ibn Abd al-Aziz Al Saud.

1982 King Khalid dies and is succeeded by his younger brother Fahd ibn Abd al-Aziz Al Saud *(below)*.

1986 A bloody coup in South Yemen results in a takeover by a hardline pro-Soviet group.

2

A sign in the store window makes clear
why the shop is closed. Until foreign
workers arrived in droves, prayer time
never had to be explained.

rest on its blood ties alone.

And as that community took shape, his own role began to grow. In Mecca he had been the religious leader of a small group. Now he was starting to play a political role, and one with widening authority. He had to keep the social fabric of his new community together, and the nature of his revelations changed accordingly, becoming more and more concrete.

Thus he introduced certain customs that he made obligatory. "Tell my servants," he conveyed from Allah, "those who are true believers, to be steadfast in prayer and to give alms in private and in public, before that day arrives when all trading shall cease and friendships be no more." He commanded that prayer be said five times a day and facing in the direction of Mecca, where the Ka'aba still exerted a pull on the hearts of his followers. He appointed one of his congregation, an Abyssinian named Bilal, who had a sonorous voice, to summon Muslims to prayer at the required times of the day. He instituted the practice of fasting during the month of Ramadan, the ninth of the lunar calendar. Concerning alms, he told the faithful by Allah's command to give "what you can spare".

It was during this period in Muhammad's life that the most specific verses in the Koran were inscribed. In addition to the religious laws governing fasting, almsgiving and daily prayer, they contain social and political ordinances dealing with marriage and divorce. In the past, Arabian men had been able to marry as many wives as they pleased—and presumably they abandoned those of whom they grew tired. The Koran condoned polygamy—but with limitations. "You may marry other women who seem

good to you: two, three, or four of them. But if you fear that you cannot maintain equality among them... marry one only or any slave-girls you may own. This will make it easier for you to avoid injustice." The Koran also permitted divorce, but again there were certain conditions: "If you wish to divorce a woman to marry another, do not take

from her the dowry you have given her." A woman was just as free as a man to initiate divorce; but if she chose to do so, she forfeited her dowry and returned to her family.

Curiously, the practice of veiling women, so conspicuous throughout the Muslim world in modern times, is nowhere mentioned in the Koran; the practice is thought to have been introduced about a century after Muhammad's death, and then not so much with the intention of shackling women as of protecting them from rough society. Most of the Koran's injunctions with respect to women were stated in a spirit of granting women justice, which was something new in Arabian society. For instance, the Koran made the practice of female infanticide—a commonplace event in the Middle East of Muhammad's day—a crime.

For more than a decade, Muhammad won adherents merely on the ap-

peal of his preaching. But in Medina he had a revelation bidding him "fight in the cause of Allah against those who fight against Him." Muhammad's position in his adopted city was secure enough, but now he resolved to carry Allah's message beyond.

Accordingly, Muhammad declared that he had been sent with the sword to lead the faithful in the destruction of all those who refused obedience to the law of Islam. Christians and Jews, who worshipped the same God–the God who had made earlier revelations to Adam, Noah, Abraham and Moses–were to be spared his wrath if they paid a head tax. But anyone who refused obedience to Islam and persisted in paganism was to be put to the sword. All who drew the sword "in the cause of the faith will be rewarded with temporal advantages," he said. "If they fall in battle they will be transported to paradise, there to revel in eternal pleasure."

Acting upon that revelation, Muhammad took to leading his followers in raids against the Meccan caravans that passed through Medina and its surrounding territory. He was, of course, adapting the age-old practice of desert raiding, and some scholars believe that he was doing so out of necessity, in order to provide his followers with the food and supplies they lacked. Others say he was avenging persecution that had been visited in Mecca on the families of his supporters. Either way, the raids on which he now embarked were mounted in the name of Allah. They constituted a holy war, the *jihad*, and pitted Muhammad and his adherents for the first time in armed conflict against his enemies.

Of several confrontations that took place, the crucial one occurred in 624 at Badr, a caravan stop 135 kilometres south-west of Medina, when Muhammad sent a force of 300 men against 1,000 men led by Quraysh from Mecca. To the surprise of everyone except perhaps himself, his men managed to inflict a crushing defeat on the Quraysh. So overwhelming had been the odds against Muhammad's followers that their victory seemed to be a miracle, a sign of God's favour towards Muhammad, and it won him more converts. Tribes from the desert now joined those from Medina in honouring him.

Periodic skirmishes between the Meccans and the Medinese ensued over the next few years. Not all of them went so stunningly in Muhammad's favour, but after the battle of Badr, he passed gradually over from the defensive to the offensive, and the Islamic faith spread rapidly.

By 630, Muhammad was ready to take on Mecca. Partly because the Meccans had lost a number of battles to Muhammad and partly because they lacked a forceful leader, they now yielded to him. After he had secured the city, he entered the Ka'aba, triumphantly exclaiming: "Truth has come and falsehood has vanished."

He was willing enough, no doubt for pragmatic reasons, to allow his followers to worship at the hallowed stone–but not to yield on the principle of only one god. With Mecca and the Ka'aba in his possession, he promptly set about destroying the many idols in the temple. Thus purified of paganism, the Ka'aba became the spiritual centre of Islam, a distinction it has maintained to the present day.

In religious matters as in politics, Muhammad demonstrated his shrewdness. Although he stripped the temple of all its idols, he left the temple intact, and he kept much of the religious

A Kuwaiti carries out his noon prayers, forehead touching the prayer mat that he usually carries rolled up with him. Muslims always pray in the direction of the holy city of Mecca.

2

ritual. He retained the practice of the annual pilgrimage, even to the circumambulation seven times around the Ka'aba. He kept the act of drinking water at the sacred Zamzam well and the pacing seven times around the area where Hagar had searched for water for Ishmael. He also kept the visit to Mount Arafat, the ritual throwing of stones at pillars representing evil spirits, and the sacrifice of camels and sheep. But whereas the camels and sheep had heretofore been slaughtered and burnt to appease a number of deities, they were now slain to honour Allah and then given to the poor for food.

If Muhammad harboured ill feelings towards his erstwhile persecutors, he overcame any such emotions when he seized Mecca, taking the magnanimous view—as a true leader must—that mercy was the wiser course. And it was. The inhabitants of Mecca fell willingly under his rule.

Thereafter, the ranks of Islam increased rapidly. By the end of 630, most of the tribes of the Hijaz, the province that runs along the northern half of the Red Sea coast, and the Najd, the province that constitutes central Arabia, were paying regular tribute to Muhammad, and converts to Islam were coming from as far away as Yemen, Oman and Bahrain. Christians and Jews in the trading cities continued to worship according to their own rites, but they paid taxes to Muhammad as political leader of the peninsula.

In the space of about two decades, Islam had spread out and Muhammad had become the most powerful leader outside the Byzantine and Persian Empires to the north and the east. He marked the occasion of the annual pilgrimage in 632 by delivering a stirring address. "O ye men! Harken unto my

words and take ye them to heart!" he said. "Know ye that every Muslim is a brother unto every other Muslim, and that ye are now one brotherhood. It is not legitimate for any one of you, therefore, to appropriate unto himself anything that belongs to his brother unless it is willingly given him by that brother."

Soon afterwards he was stricken with a fever, headaches and other symptoms that modern historians believe to have been caused by pneumonia. He died within a few days of his sermon.

So despairing were his intimates that some of them thought news of his death should be kept from the people. But Abu Bakr, who had been among Muhammad's earliest confidants and more recently had become his father-in-law, intervened with wise counsel: "Whichever of you worships Muhammad, know that Muhammad is dead. But whichever of you worships God, know that God is alive and does not die." He then quoted a verse from the Koran, reminding his listeners: "He is a Prophet only; there have been prophets before him. If he dies or is slain, will ye turn back?"

Abu Bakr's well-chosen words stemmed what might have turned into a panic, but they left unsolved the troublesome problem of succession. Muhammad had not designated anyone to take his place, and as is often the case when a great leader leaves a vacuum, his followers could not agree on a successor. The Quraysh who had migrated with him to Medina insisted that a kinsman should succeed. The Muslims of Medina argued that—as the Prophet himself had proclaimed—all Muslims were brothers, and that the caliph (Arabic for "successor") to the Prophet should be elected from among the ranks of all believers.

Of the many contenders for the role, four in particular stood out. The first of these was the sensible Abu Bakr. Two others were Umar and Uthman, men who had been Muhammad's early associates and longtime advisers. The fourth was Ali, who staked his claim on the fact that he was the next of kin. As the son of Muhammad's uncle Abu Talib, he was a first cousin of the Prophet; more recently he had become a son-in-law, having married Muhammad's daughter Fatima and fathered the Prophet's only two grandsons.

For practicality's sake all the contenders but Ali put aside their own aspirations and settled on Abu Bakr by acclamation. Ali temporarily left the political arena, but his adherents–who came to be called Shiat Ali, meaning "Partisans of Ali", and later simply Shia or Shiites–persisted in the conviction that Ali alone was the rightful caliph of Muhammad.

The rift initiated by Ali's supporters was to survive into the modern era. A number of minor groups have arisen from time to time over the ages, but to this day Islam continues to be divided chiefly into those two factions: Shiites, who claim descent from the Prophet via Ali and Fatima's progeny, and Sunni, who believe that the leader should be selected from among those who best demonstrate personal character and a knowledge of the Koran.

During the reign of Abu Bakr, Muslim warriors started to press the cause of Islam beyond the Arabian Peninsula, north into Syria and east into Iraq. Abu Bakr did not live to see the results of their fighting; he died in 634. Umar was the next to be acclaimed Commander of the Faithful. During the 10 years of his reign, the transformation of Islam from a local state into a world-

A South Yemen woman doctor makes home visits by motorcycle, yet bows to tradition by wearing a veil in public.

2

wide empire began. By the year 640, Muslim soldiers under his leadership held sway over the whole of Syria, had conquered Egypt and Iraq, and were gaining control of Persia.

In spite of those impressive military victories and political gains, Muslims everywhere were beset by personal and tribal jealousies, particularly as the conquests spread. One unhappy warrior who felt he had been slighted murdered Umar in 644.

The next Commander of the Faithful was Uthman, who reigned for 12 years. His rule saw the beginning of Muslim expansion into North Africa in 648 and the completion of the conquest of Persia in 651. Closer to home, however, he made enemies who claimed that he favoured kinsmen at the expense of the broader interests of the community of Islam. As bickering among the faithful increased, Ali resurfaced in Medina and rallied sympathizers, who asserted Uthman was unfit to rule. In 656, an angry mob stormed into the old man's house and murdered him while he was reciting the Koran. The mob then promptly acclaimed Ali as caliph and Commander of the Faithful.

Ali's own position was by no means secure, however, and he had no sooner gained the leadership he had so long coveted than he left Medina to establish himself in Iraq, where his chief support lay. Only 24 years after the death of Muhammad, the centre of Islamic political rule was moving out of the Arabian Peninsula. Medina was never again to be the political capital of Islam. Henceforth the course of Islamic history (as distinct from the history of the Arabian Peninsula) was to be directed from elsewhere.

Meanwhile, the essential message endured. The entire religion can be summed up in five simple words: faith, prayer, almsgiving, fasting and pilgrimage—five ritual obligations that are known to Muslims as the five pillars of Islam. The first pillar is *shahada*, the mere profession of faith: "There is no god but Allah, and Muhammad is his messenger," which, when said in Arabic, is wonderfully alliterative—*la ilaha illa Allah; Muhammad rasul Allah.* That invocation is intoned over every newborn Muslim infant, over the grave of every corpse, and at least five times daily as part of the call to prayer. The mere utterance of the phrase is enough to make a person a Muslim; no other ritual is necessary.

The second pillar is *salat*, the prayers that follow that invocation five times daily. Prayers consist of verses from the Koran, wherein the name of God is mentioned repeatedly. Prayers may be said in solitude or in company, but at noon on Fridays they are said publicly in a mosque. There the imam, the local leader chosen by acclamation for his learnedness and piety, delivers a sermon and leads the congregation in prayer, but he does so as an equal of his brother Muslims, not in the role of a priestly intercessor. This requisite weekly congregation has been essential to promoting the brotherhood of the faithful, which in theory—if not always in fact—takes precedence over any blood relationships.

The third pillar is *zakat*, the giving of 2.5 per cent of accumulated wealth as alms. In the early days, Islamic officials took cattle, corn, fruit and merchandise belonging to the prosperous faithful and dispensed it to the poor; once currency gained a foothold, a monetary tax was substituted.

The fourth pillar is *sawm*, ritual fasting every day during the month of Ramadan. That month may have been sacred in pre-Islamic days; the Koran deems it holy because it was during Ramadan that Muhammad was first inspired with the word of Allah, and again in Ramadan that the victory of Badr was won. From dawn till sunset during the entire month, abstinence from all food and drink and from sexual relations is required of every Muslim. The fasting imposes self-discipline on all Muslims and at the same time gives them a penitential feeling for the plight of the poor. Even so, Ramadan is a favourite month among them; after sundown they feast, and the mosques are lit all night.

The fifth and final pillar of Islam is the *hajj*, the pilgrimage. Once in a lifetime every Muslim of either sex is expected to undertake a visit to Mecca and there must follow prescribed rituals *(pages 52-59)*. In the years since Muhammad's death, the *hajj* has had much to do with binding together the brotherhood of Islam from all over the world—and everything to do with keeping the Arabian Peninsula alive in the minds of Muslims in the centuries when politically and economically it sank into near oblivion.

The injunction to spread the faith—by sword point, if necessary—is sometimes called the sixth pillar of Islam. In the centuries since Muhammad first led his Medinese followers against the Meccans, holy war—the *jihad*—has been repeatedly waged to enlarge the realm of true belief and return nonbelievers and backsliders into the fold.

Muhammad's weaning his contemporaries from freewheeling idolatry and his success in inducing the fiercely independent Arabians to obey his social ordinances together represent one of the most remarkable accomplish-

A Yemeni studies the Koran in his local mosque. Glimmering behind him are the inscribed tiles and brass decorations of the *kiblah*, a niche that is built into every mosque to indicate the direction of Mecca.

ments in all of history. His revolution gave the Arabian people a sense of unity they had never known before and a spirit that made them capable of expanding their frontiers.

The explanation for his success lies partly in the fact that Islam's message was straightforward and practical. It was unencumbered by complex theology, and it swept away the contradictory superstitions of the pagan age. Its proclamation of God's will and of the need to submit made consummate good sense to a people accustomed to making the best of life in an implacable desert—where co-operation was the important key to survival.

Furthermore, Islam's demands for charity and its provisions for justice of-

fered much-needed hope to the poor and the downtrodden, while at the same time giving the prosperous ruling classes of the caravan cities a new sense of responsibility towards their less fortunate neighbours. Finally, in stressing that all Muslims were brothers, Muhammad had emphasized the positive aspects of the family, thereby striking a resonant chord in a society that was already family-minded.

For all those reasons, Muhammad had called forth a social grouping that was united as never before. That sense of unity would survive—despite internecine raiding, despite incessant migrations—among the Bedouin, who for the next 1,200 years constituted the backbone of the Arabian Peninsula.

During the annual *hajj*, Muslims stream into the marble-walled Great Mosque, whose flat roof is also used for prayer.

ACT OF MASS DEVOTION

For a few weeks each year, Saudi Arabia is host to a stupendous flow of the faithful: they come to fulfil the Koranic commandment that each Muslim shall at least once in his or her lifetime make the Great Pilgrimage, or *hajj*, to Mecca. In the past, pilgrims, or *hajjis*, sometimes spent months and even years on their journey to the Holy City. Now, thanks to jet travel, Muslims from anywhere in the world can accomplish the *hajj* in a single week.

Altogether, more than 1.5 million pilgrims a year make their way to the Great Mosque, a vast structure built by the Saudis in the first flush of the oil boom. There the *hajjis* perform some of the complicated rites of the pilgrimage, including the seven circumambulations of the Ka'aba, the stone structure in the courtyard of the mosque, and the saluting or kissing of the Black Stone embedded in the Ka'aba. The climax of the *hajj* is the *wuoof* or "standing"–an extraordinary act of mass devotion that takes place not in Mecca itself but 19 kilometres east, on the plain of Mount Arafat.

Hajjis arrive at Jidda airport wearing the traditional garment: two pieces of seamless white cloth, one wrapped around the lower body, the other simply draped over the torso. In dressing alike, the pilgrims symbolize their equality before God.

Pilgrims pray facing the Ka'aba, a cube-shaped structure covered in gold-embroidered black cloth.

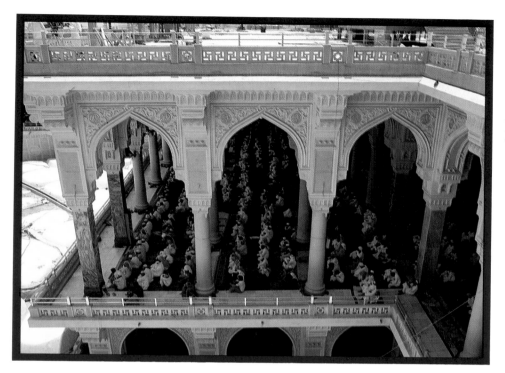

Orderly ranks of the faithful gather on a balcony in the Great Mosque, which has colonnades on two levels and can contain 500,000 worshippers.

Hajjis take part in the *s'ay* or "running"—seven circuits between the hills of Safa and Marwa—along a 420-metre tiled corridor with a central aisle for pilgrims in wheelchairs.

Chanting "At your call, O God, I come here," devout Muslims blanket Mount Arafat, site of the Prophet's last sermon. The ceremony of the standing—which lasts from noon to sunset—is the focus of the *hajj*; failure to perform it properly nullifies the entire pilgrimage.

Hajjis crowd round a circular pit to throw stones at a pillar symbolizing Satan. The ritual—which shows their determination to resist temptation—requires pilgrims to stone three such pillars with a total of 49 pebbles.

A cook prepares an enormous vat of rice and roast fowl for the Feast of Sacrifice, which marks the end of the Great Pilgrimage. As part of the celebration, each pilgrim shows his or her willingness to sacrifice for God by sacrificing an animal.

After the sacrifice, a *hajji* has a ritual haircut; only three hairs need be cut, but many men have their heads shaved.

WANDERERS OF THE DESERT

The Bedouin, the nomadic camel herders of the Arabian Peninsula, care little for boundaries, wandering freely across them as they tend their animals. And so it happened one day, according to a tale told around Bedouin camp-fires, that authorities of the Syrian desert arrested a Bedouin of the Rwala tribe who had wandered into its territory. By Bedouin standards, his detention was outrageous and an affront to family honour. The sheikh–head of the man's extended family–tried to secure the prisoner's release by reasoning with the authorities, but his arguments did not avail. So the sheikh's eight-year-old son undertook to settle the matter himself. Armed with a penknife and aided by a few friends his own age, he tried to steal into the prison to free his kinsman.

The would-be rescuers were not successful, but such an effort by mere children to help a fellow tribesman speaks volumes about the Bedouin society and the Bedouin view of what is proper behaviour. The principle of the matter was simple: by Bedouin tradition that goes back several centuries , a slight to any particular individual is considered a slight to that person's kin–his tribe. It used to be that the aggrieved tribal group would seek retribution by raiding the tribe that had committed the offence and seizing its camels. "I against my brothers, I and my brothers against my cousins; but I, my brothers and my cousins against the world," runs an old desert proverb.

Raiding has now passed into history. In 1932, after founding the Kingdom of Saudi Arabia, Abd al-Aziz ibn Saud made keeping the peace and dispensing justice the state's functions, and the peninsula's other sovereign nations have followed suit. But the sentiments underlying raiding–tribal loyalty, bravery, honour and solidarity, and the involvement of each and every member of the tribe in upholding those traditional values–continue to permeate every corner of Arabian society. Fully three quarters of today's inhabitants of the peninsula–including the ruling families of Saudi Arabia and most of the coastal states–proudly claim descent from the Bedouin.

Until the early years of the 20th century, the Bedouin were a major political and military force in the Arabian Peninsula. As camel herders, they supplied pack animals to the caravan trade that brought the land wealth. As nomads, they patrolled the trade routes and gave military protection to the caravan cities. In return for these services they exacted payment in the form of rice, dates, clothing, jewellery, coffee pots and bowls made of copper and brass, and swords and rifles.

With governments now enforcing the peace, and with the peninsula's wealth counted in oil barrels rather than in camels, no village needs protection by the Bedouin, and no market needs their camels to transport cargo. The Bedouin have therefore lost most of their political strength.

But they have not fallen out of favour. Though many citified Arabians working in the high-rise office buildings of Jidda, Riyadh, Kuwait City and Doha affect to look down upon present-day nomads as being unshod, illiterate, unruly, ill-fed and unkempt primitives, the same workers nevertheless praise the legendary Bedouin courage and fighting prowess. And they will cite verses from epic Arabic poetry to prove their point, until, as one Western observer reports, "the hungry, ragged men whom they had just been reviling" are transformed into "the legendary heroes of the past".

Among the Bedouin themselves, neither shoelessness nor illiteracy is any cause for shame. Every Bedouin tribesman counts himself the equal of any person alive–including the ruler. A visiting Englishman once asked a group of Bedouin who had returned from a mission to King Abd al-Aziz ibn Saud what form of address they had used in his presence. The question astonished them. "We called him Abd al-Aziz," they declared. "How else should we call him except by his name?"

"I thought you might call him 'Your Majesty,' " the Englishman explained.

"We are Bedouin," they answered.

"We have no king but God."

By strict definition, a Bedouin is a desert nomad who speaks Arabic, lives in a tent, raises camels and belongs to a tribe. No one knows how many of the Bedouin fit that definition today. Estimates range between 200,000 and 300,000, or less than 1 per cent of the population. Exact figures are hard to come by, partly because tribal grazing areas spill casually across national boundaries, and partly because today's Bedouin are increasingly giving up camel herding to use the car and truck

Separated from the men's section of the tent by dividers, Bedouin women tend their children. One baby lies unseen in a leather cradle slung from the standing mother's shoulder.

3

for transportation in the desert. They are also giving up their portable tents for permanent dwellings of sun-dried clay or even cement.

Some have taken to tilling the soil, growing fruits and vegetables in oasis settlements, and herding sheep and goats. Others have moved into cities to take jobs as taxi drivers and to oil fields to work at drilling and hauling. Jobs such as these appeal to the Bedouin because they provide them with the opportunity to move around and hence preserve an illusion of the traditional Bedouin mobility.

Yet–compounding the problem of numbering them–many of those who succumb to the lure of modern jobs

continue to think of themselves as Bedouin. One Western visitor tells of hitching a ride with a Bedouin youth employed as a truck driver for one of the oil companies: "He drives us with wild abandon over the rough road, happy to be going home 'to my tent', as he calls it. His 'tent' turns out to be an air-conditioned Winnebago camper-van with a battery-operated television set inside." Yet the youth proudly insisted he was still a Bedouin.

The key to that frame of mind is an intricate web of relationships that ties every Bedouin to an extended family: a *fakhida*, consisting of cousins down to the fifth generation; a *fakhd* (branch of a tribe), made up of several *fakhidas*; and

ultimately a tribe, which can trace its history to a common ancestor.

There are some 60 tribes scattered throughout the peninsula. The larger counts thousands of members. The Rwala, who trace their lineage back to Muhammad's tribe, the Quraysh, have been estimated at more than 30,000 strong. They owe their pre-eminence not just to their control of specific wells and grazing areas, but to the size of the camel herds that their ancestors once possessed, to their long-gone role in protecting trading and to their ancient prowess at fighting.

Few tribes command more respect than the Al Murrah, though it has only about 15,000 members. The Al Murrah steadfastly persists in migrating over a swath of territory that runs 965 kilometres along the northern fringe of the forbidding Rub'al-Khali, from the border of Kuwait in the north-east to the oasis of Jabrin in southern Saudi Arabia. In the face of the modern trend towards raising sheep and goats, the Al Murrah still herds only camels—some of the finest camels to be found anywhere in the world.

An archetypal member of the tribe is Ali ibn Salim al-Kurbi, a lean, grey-bearded patriarch who is past the age of 70. Within the Al Murrah tribe he belongs to a branch known as Al Azab, and within that branch to a further subdivision, the Al Kurbi *fakhida*, named after an ancestor five generations back. Altogether the Al Kurbi numbers 64 men, women and children in nine households.

With Ali live his wife, two sons, one married and one single, a daughter-in-law (who is also his niece because Ali's son abided by custom and married his cousin), and a son of that marriage. By Bedouin standards, Ali's household is fairly prosperous. It maintains a herd of 60 or more camels, nearly three times the number kept by families the size of his. Some of the female camels keep the family supplied with milk, while others serve for breeding. Still more camels carry the Bedouin themselves, and others their belongings.

Ali's family possessions include a goat-hair tent 12 metres long and open along the front—the side facing south, away from the prevailing north-north-westerly winds. The tent is divided inside by a curtain that separates the men's quarters from the women's. Among the other family possessions are some hand-woven rugs, brass and enamel cooking utensils, wooden camel

A Bedouin driver rests in the shade beneath his truck at midday. Bedouin love driving, perhaps because it seems an extension of their old nomadic life—depicted here on the truck door.

3

saddles with sheepskin coverings, leather saddlebags, goatskin bags for hauling water, a coil of rope, and a couple of moisture-proof metal boxes for storing the few luxuries the family allows itself, such as frankincense and sandalwood for ritual burning.

The family's clothing is as spare as its household goods. The men wear a loose-fitting, ankle-length gown called a *thawb*, which buttons at the neck like a nightshirt and is made of white cotton. It serves as something of an air conditioner, for when the wearer moves around, he sets up convection currents that cool him. The male headdress, or *ghutra*, is a large square of cotton cloth (red and white checks in Ali's family) draped and folded about the head to give protection from dust, heat and flies. It is worn over a cotton skull-cap and often held in place by a double cord wrapped around the head.

The men's principal ornament is their weaponry. Every adult male in Ali's family sports a silver dagger and an intricately decorated Yemeni-made cartridge belt filled with bullets—status symbols that are too expensive for poorer Bedouin.

The men also take pains with their grooming. They affect flowing hair, shoulder-length or longer; or they braid it, a style favoured by traditional desert Bedouin as being particularly manly and attractive to women. By contrast, long hair is frowned upon in the cities, where men wear it short.

The women's clothes are elaborately decorous. Over white gauze blouses and pantaloons that completely cover their legs, Ali's wife and daughter-in-law wear multicoloured long-sleeved dresses and black cloaks that reach to their feet. Their hair is concealed under black kerchiefs. They sometimes rub a heavy black cosmetic, kohl, around their eyes, which serves to emphasize the eyes and also absorbs the glare of the desert sun. However, for modesty's sake, they drape their faces in black veils with the merest eyeslits for looking out. Yielding to a taste for extravagance, they adorn themselves with gold and silver rings set with turquoise, onyx, garnets or carnelians; and they may wear 10 or even 20 bracelets on each arm. The wealthier the head of a desert family is, the more bejewelled will be his womenfolk, who thus display his generosity.

For a nomadic family such as Ali's, life is a constant search for water and grazing. For much of the year, their travelling is done in short stints over distances that amount to approximately 10 kilometres every few days. But twice a year, in early winter and in late spring, the whole tribe will undertake major migrations from one end of its territory to the other so that the herd of camels may flourish.

In December and January, from a point somewhere inside the Rub'al-Khali, Ali's sons and nephews and the other tribesmen scan the horizon daily for rain clouds, which will be the signal that the time has arrived for the tribe's winter migration. This involves a long march north towards the Kuwait border. Here, reliable winter rains ensure that the desert's sparse vegetation turn green. The grazing grounds are available to all comers on a first-come-first-served basis.

For Ali, his household and their 60 camels, the journey amounts to a 650-kilometre dash that has to be accomplished within a period of 10 days or two weeks in order not to miss a single day of good grazing. Once they reach their destination, there is time to

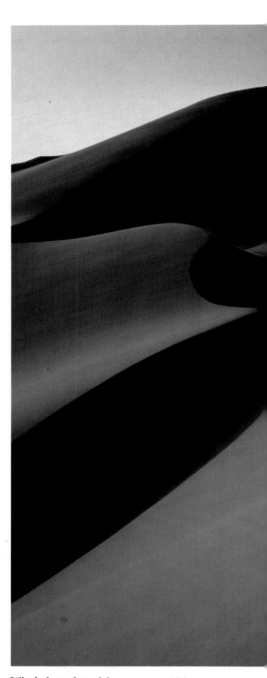

Wind-shaped sand dunes soar to 150 metres in the Rub'al-Khali, or Empty Quarter, the desert of southern Arabia. Bedouin are appropriately named for such austere terrain: *badiya* is Arabic for "desert", and *badawiyin* means "inhabitants of the desert".

An Al Murrah woman joins her clan in a migration to fresh pastures, carrying on her camel a goat whose milk is used mainly for making butter. The saluki hound trailing behind is a Bedouin favourite, used to catch hares for the cooking pot.

relax and enjoy the company of others.

The Al Murrah shares the grazing grounds with the Ajman, Mutayr, Dawasir, Subai and other tribes—erstwhile rivals whose camps they used to raid. Nowadays, feasting and intermingling go on. Occasionally there may even be visits from members of the royal family, who take pride in their Bedouin descent and like to keep in touch with the ancient ways.

Ali and his kin travel about the region in small family groups, making camp with half a dozen or more other household tents; once in a while, all 35 households of the Al Azab branch camp together. When they do, they share herding, prayers and meals, taking turns to eat in one another's tents.

There is no set pattern to their congregating or to their moves. Any household may remain in one spot for a day or two and then shift to a new location a few kilometres away, wherever the grass is fresh and green. Browsing on juicy pasturage, the camels fatten, their humps swelling with stored nourishment. It is during this period that the calves are born.

By February the rains have stopped. In late March the temperature begins to rise, climbing as high as 32°C, and sandstorms blow up. When the plants begin to shrivel and turn brown, usually in April, Ali and his household start moving again in the direction of the Rub'al-Khali. There is no reason to hurry this time. They set out for any of several wells where the Al Murrah has usage rights because, as they explain, "our ancestors owned them" before the time of Muhammad.

The Al Azab branch of the tribe congregates in the Rub'al-Khali in the vicinity of Jabrin, about 240 kilometres south-east of Riyadh. Here the families

spend the summer, in enervating heat. Their main occupation is to milk the camels—which in summer yield only once in four days—and to haul up well water for the animals. (At this time of year the camels must drink every three days; in winter, when the air is much cooler and vegetation contains more moisture, they can go without drinking for days on end.) There are no pastures to drive the herds to; the camels are on their own to chew whatever stubble they can find and to survive on the fat stored in their humps.

In autumn the families start drifting from the interior to the edge of the desert again, in order to be ready for the winter dash for pasturage. When they reach the point from which they started the year before, they will have travelled at least 1,900 kilometres and perhaps a good many more.

Throughout this odyssey, the daily routine varies little from one place to another. The day begins at dawn with a call to prayer, which is usually delivered by Ali himself or, in his absence, by the oldest son present. The men stroll out of the tent—male guests and

A member of the Al Kurbi family of the Al Murrah tribe wears a white, lightweight headdress in place of the thicker red and white patterned *ghutra*. Reluctant to give up their nomadic life, the Al Murrah have been called "the Arabs of the Arabs".

unmarried youths from the men's side, and the married men from the women's section, where they have spent the night with their wives. Bending over the sand and facing in the direction of Mecca, someone draws an arc that represents a mosque's prayer niche. Each man gives his face a ritual splash of cleansing water—or goes through the motions with a sprinkling of sand—and the ancient chant begins: "*Allah akbar, Allah akbar*" ("God is great, God is great"). Inside the tent, the women also face towards Mecca, but they say their prayers silently.

The chanting ends as the sun breaks over the horizon, and the women rekindle the previous night's fire by throwing twigs from desert bushes or dried camel dung on the embers. Soon there comes the rhythmic sound of fresh-roasted coffee beans being pounded, the stone pestle hitting the side of the brass mortar like the clapper of a bell as though to summon the camp for breakfast. The meal is spare—a few dates, a bowl of camel's milk, perhaps a thin slab of unleavened bread that has been cooked in the embers of the coffee fire.

Over coffee the men discuss the day's activities. Should they stay put and graze the camels nearby, or is it time to move on? At least one of the men will have spent the previous day scouting the surrounding area on camelback to judge the quality of the grazing and the availability of water.

Periodically, members of the Royal Saudi National Guard appear in trucks, telling of good pasturage they have seen. (One Bedouin, when asked how he knew about rainfall in distant pastures, replied, "News reaches us on the backs of Datsuns.")

If the men decide to stay where they are, the herd will be divided into

groups. One man will take the she-camels with young calves to the grazing area nearest the tent, where they can be given fullest attention. He must see that these mothers drink water at least once a week, even in winter, to stay in milk. They are the most highly prized because they give the sweetest milk and the milk provides much of the Bedouin's nourishment. To make sure that the baby camels do not take all, the Al Azab ties knitted woollen protectors on the mother's udders.

Females with older calves are led farther away, generally by one of the younger men. If he expects to have to go a long way, he may be mounted on a riding camel. In years of bountiful rain, when he does not have to go far, he returns with the camels at nightfall; in dry years, when grass cover is sparse, he may keep them out a week or more before returning to camp. The remaining camels are allowed to forage on their own in the vicinity of the camp, but they are hobbled to prevent them from straying too far.

While the men are out herding or scouting the desert in quest for new grazing, the women attend to chores at camp—collecting firewood, mending clothes, fetching water if there is a well nearby, perhaps weaving the brightly patterned fabric partitions that divide their side of the tent from the men's. The children who are five or younger mill about the campsite, the boys wrestling or running foot races, the girls miming their mothers at keeping the tent in order. Up to this age, boys and girls sometimes mingle. But after they have reached the age of five or six, both sexes begin helping with the work; the boys accompany the menfolk who go out with the herds, and the girls learn such tasks as churning butter, carding wool and weaving.

In the pastures and at the tent alike, all work stops at noon for prayers, after which everyone naps–the herders in the spidery shade of a desert shrub while the camels settle down to chew their cud. The afternoon passes in much the same way as the morning, and two hours before sunset, prayers are said again. When at last the late-afternoon winds blow up, it is time for those who are close by to return with the animals to camp. More prayers are said at sunset, fires are lit to make cof-

ORNAMENTS FOR WEARERS OF THE VEIL

A Bedouin woman's jewellery is adornment, economic status symbol and badge of fecundity: new pieces are the reward for bearing sons. A woman will wear several pieces at a time, from headpieces, necklaces and bracelets to rings on her fingers and her toes. Most Bedouin jewellery is decorated with soldered metal strips, intricate filigree and inlaid glass or stones. Highly prized pieces are crafted by Najrani and Yemeni silversmiths, some of whose work is shown here.

Traditionally, certain shapes and numerical configurations of amulets, chains and beads have talismanic significance. Triangles and crescents are thought to offer protection against the evil eye. Hand shapes—or combinations of five amulets, the numerical equivalent of the hand— represent the five most important Islamic tenets.

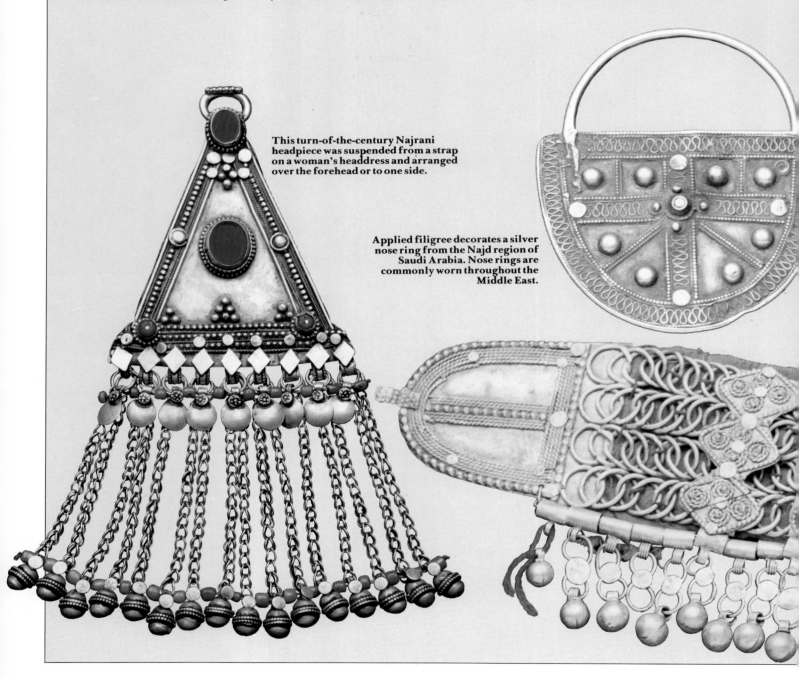

This turn-of-the-century Najrani headpiece was suspended from a strap on a woman's headdress and arranged over the forehead or to one side.

Applied filigree decorates a silver nose ring from the Najd region of Saudi Arabia. Nose rings are commonly worn throughout the Middle East.

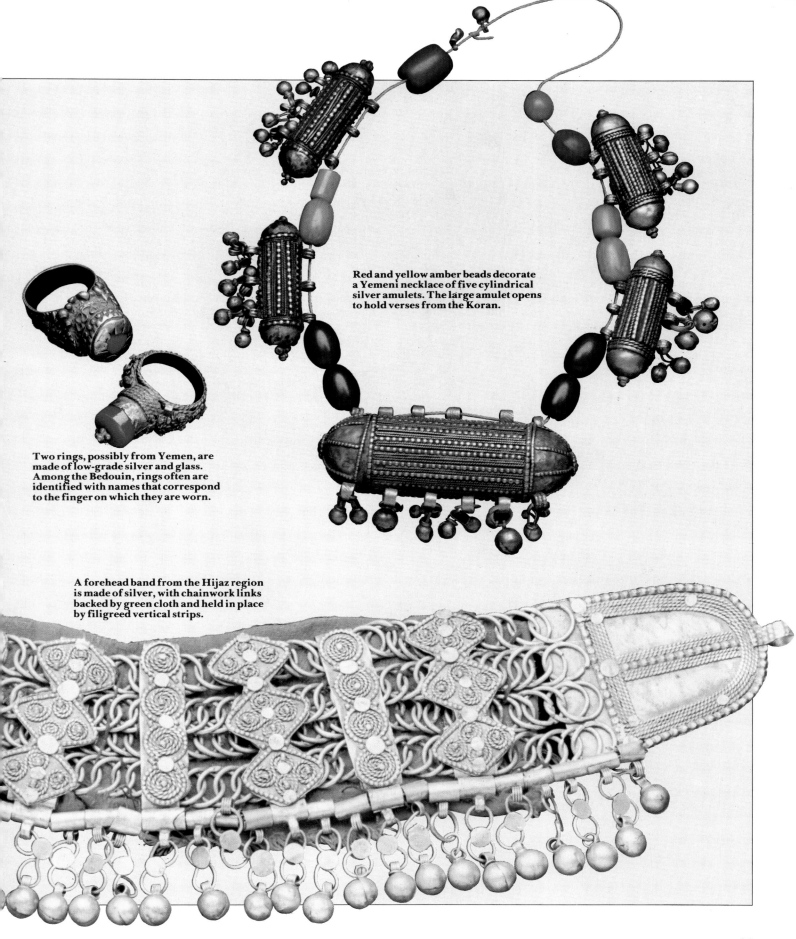

Red and yellow amber beads decorate a Yemeni necklace of five cylindrical silver amulets. The large amulet opens to hold verses from the Koran.

Two rings, possibly from Yemen, are made of low-grade silver and glass. Among the Bedouin, rings often are identified with names that correspond to the finger on which they are worn.

A forehead band from the Hijaz region is made of silver, with chainwork links backed by green cloth and held in place by filigreed vertical strips.

3

fee, and the camels are milked.

Milking a large herd like Ali's takes several hours, and it is generally a man's job. First, the milker scours the enamel milk bowl with sand. He removes the woollen protectors from the camels' udders and allows the calves to suckle for a while. When he is ready to start milking, he goes into an elaborate balancing act, bracing his right foot against the left knee and cradling the milk bowl in his lap as he holds the bowl up under the camel. He strokes her udder, encouraging the animal to let down her milk, and goes to work. A healthy, well-fed camel that has calved within the year will produce as much as 4 litres a day.

Some hours after sunset, when the camels have been milked and bedded down and the final prayers have been said, the camp assembles for dinner. The men gather around the coffee fire on their side of the tent and someone fetches a platter of boiled rice from the women's quarters, where it has been cooked. If some lucky herder has shot a hare or other game during the day, it will have been skinned, boiled and added to the rice platter. But usually the meal consists solely of rice, perhaps moistened with clarified butter and sometimes a few onions. The men squat together around the platter, kneading the rice into pellets with their right hand and then tossing the pellets into their mouth. Their left hand, which is used for wiping themselves after defecating and for blowing their nose and is thus considered to be tainted, is kept hidden throughout the meal within the folds of their robe.

The men take care to leave some food on the platter for the women and eventually pass it back to them to finish. The diners clean their hands by rubbing them in sand to remove the grease. Then the men relax around the fire, drinking tiny cups of bitter coffee flavoured with cardamom.

Once again the conversation revolves around the camel. For the camel is not only the family's most prized possession; it is means of transportation, larder and (by converting pasturage into milk) water purification plant all in one, and hence the linchpin of human life in the desert.

To Westerners who have encountered it, the camel is a beast of foul breath and notoriously bad temper. But the Bedouin man loves his camels with a passion. He kisses them, calls them by name, makes up poems about them. What is more, the camel may return his affection. The British explorer Wilfred Thesiger wrote of a she-camel that "was as attached to her owner as a dog might have been. At intervals throughout the night she came over, moaning softly, to sniff at him where he lay, before going back to graze. My companions told me that no one else could ride her unless he took with him a piece of her owner's clothing."

Such intimacy is the result of long association and early training. From a very young age, boys and girls alike are taught how to recognize the footprints of each individual animal that belongs to their family's herd.

The tracking abilities of a seasoned nomad are positively uncanny. Even when the spoor is unfamiliar, the Bedouin can tell the camel's sex, whether or not it was being ridden, whether pregnant, where it had been grazing, when it had last been watered. The depth of the footprint indicates whether the beast was carrying a rider or baggage—and thus determines the sex: riding camels are females because they have a gentler gait; pack animals are bulls because they can carry loads of up to 180 kilograms. If the footprints show the impress of loose strips of skin, the Bedouin knows that the camels have come from the sands; if the prints are smooth, that they have come from the gravel plains, which polish footpads hard and smooth.

By examining camel droppings, the Bedouin can determine what kind of vegetation the beast has consumed; the moisture or dryness of the droppings tells him how long ago it passed that way. Finally, the pattern of the tracks betrays the camel driver's mission; a herd marching towards winter pasturage makes one complex of tracks, while a herd grazing desultorily makes another. In the old days, stolen camels that were hurried home by raiders made different tracks from those of a heavily laden merchant caravan.

Thesiger, riding across the Rub'al-Khali in the 1950s, once came across some camel tracks that were practically obliterated by the wind. One of the Bedouin guides travelling with him dismounted to examine them. The guide studied the tracks, picked up some of the camel droppings and broke them between his fingers. After thinking a moment, he said, "They were Awamir. There were six of them. They have raided the Junuba on the southern coast and taken three of their camels. They passed here ten days ago."

A month later, Thesiger's party encountered some other desert travellers and, on exchanging their news, learnt that the tracker had been correct in every particular.

In a land so desolate that a month or more may go by without any human contact beyond the immediate family, life is gruelling in the best of times. In

SECRETS OF THE CAMEL

Brought to pasture in a truck by its Bedouin master, a camel preserves the hauteur of its species.

The camel is a nasty animal. It kicks, bites and spits–and whines when a load is placed on its back. Worse, perhaps, it resists commands. Yet the tribes of the Arabian Peninsula could not have survived without it. For more than 3,000 years the camel has been their beast of burden and means of transport, as well as source of food, leather and wool. And despite its disposition, the Arabs came to love it.

The camel is perfectly adapted to its desert environment. Not only can it shut its nostrils against wind-blown sand, but it can flick away any grains that get in its eyes with a pair of third eyelids. Leathery pads on its feet keep it from sinking into sand. And a remarkable digestive system enables it to eat just about anything, including leather, cloth and bone. The interior of its mouth is so tough that even thorns will not puncture the walls, and its stomach acts as a fermenting vat where bacteria break down all it swallows.

Against lean days, the camel stores fat–not water–in its hump. As the fat is depleted, the hump shrinks and flops to one side. The camel's ability to go without water for days at a time is due to a unique mechanism. Its temperature rises during the hottest part of the day, and the heat is retained in its body; thus moisture that would go into the manufacture of sweat to cool the animal is conserved. At night the excess heat is released. Still, the camel may lose up to 30 per cent of its weight through dehydration. One long drink is all it needs to put the weight back on.

3

years of drought the situation can be disastrous. "A cloud gathers, rain falls, men live; the cloud disperses without rain, and men and animals die," is how Thesiger put it.

Food is always scarce, meat is a rarity, and the average daily intake of camel's milk, dates and rice amounts only to 2,000 calories–barely enough for basic nutrition. Wells sometimes dry up, and even when they do not the water is frequently foul and alkaline. Some years, swarms of locusts strip the desert of its meagre growth, and even though the Bedouin catch and eat them, the insects hardly make up for the lost milk from starving camels. The average life span for inhabitants of the desert is between 40 and 45 years.

Such an environment might have made the Bedouin self-pitying, stingy and mean, but quite the opposite is true. There are few people on earth as lavishly hospitable as they. Should a visitor–even a stranger–arrive at a nomad's tent, the owner will give him a warm welcome and offer to slaughter a sheep or a young camel–no matter how scarce meat may be. If the host has nothing on hand but coffee and a few dates, he will serve them to his guest nonetheless, even if it means that he himself must go hungry.

When the guest is a fellow tribesman, the sense of occasion can be overwhelming. Once Ali, returning from Mecca with a party that included other members of the Al Kurbi and an American friend, happened upon the camp of a kinsman whom he had not seen for months. The kinsman's 20-year-old son Hurran, the first to spot the travellers as they approached the encampment, came rushing out of his tent to bid them a tearful welcome. "He kissed the old man Ali and the Al

Kurbi and all of us one by one," the American recorded.

"By Allah, you will eat meat," Hurran said between sobs, and he turned to run into the desert to fetch a camel.

Ali, thinking to let common sense prevail over tradition at a camp where the herd was small, stopped him. "By Allah, Hurran, we will not," he said.

"It's been half a year and we've been in the desert and we haven't seen anyone. By Allah you must eat," the young herdsman rejoined.

"Listen, my son," Ali insisted. "We are all one; your house and my house are one and our herds are one."

Because of the old man's insistence, Hurran acceded. But his impulsive generosity was typical of a sentiment that is instilled in the soul of every Bedouin from babyhood.

In a sense, generosity is an adaptive

A Yam tribesman displays a *dabb*, a heavy desert lizard, destined for the camp's supper platter. Any protein is welcome in the Bedouin's meat-scarce diet, including raw or roasted locusts.

response to an extraordinarily difficult environment. Particularly in times past, a traveller in the sandy wastes needed all the co-operation he could get, or else he would perish. His host was honour-bound to feed and clothe him and–if he had been robbed of his camels or in some other way been the victim of foul play–to defend him to the death against further attack. And should the wayfarer lose any goods or chattel during his stay, the host would be obliged to replace them. After three days, the host would see the traveller safely on his way with presents of clothing and food to sustain him.

Many rituals of desert hospitality have persisted unchanged for centuries. When a guest arrives, he is seated on the rug and the coffee fire is lit. A boy generally takes charge of brewing and serving. While the water boils, he roasts the beans lightly in a long-handled skillet and then pulverizes them in a heavy brass mortar. He pours the powder into a long-beaked brass or copper coffee pot along with boiling water from the kettle, and sets the pot on the fire to boil up again.

The brewer then calls to one of the women for cardamom seeds, which he grinds in the mortar and adds to the coffee. A platter of dates is handed across the tent divider for the boy to pass around, first to the guest and then to everyone else according to age. Then he serves the coffee, having tested it first for flavour.

With the pot in his left hand and a stack of tiny porcelain cups in his right, he moves around the group, filling each cup about one quarter full and proffering it to one person after another. He circles again to pour refills until each drinker wiggles his cup to indicate he has had enough. If the family is well-to-

do or the visitor a special one, a dish of incense or smoking sandalwood is usually passed round after the coffee cups have been collected. Everyone takes a bracing whiff—an agreeable custom that chases away the odours of the tent. If the visitor has come to do business, the men deal with it when the coffee and incense are finished.

Bedouin women seldom stay as secluded as their urban counterparts, and if the visitor is a kinsman or known by everybody, they will drift back and forth between the men's and the women's sections of the tent. Should a visitor arrive when all the men are absent, a woman will serve the coffee and entertain him.

The nomad's compulsive hospita-lity, while enhancing his honour and status, tends to keep him poor. One of the most respected tribesmen in southern Arabia in the 1950s was an elder of the Bayt Imani tribe. In his prime he had been rich in camels, but over the years he had slaughtered his entire herd to feed the guests that came his way. In ancient times such a man would simply have replaced the animals by raiding another tribe's herd. That being no longer possible, the elder was broken by his own generosity, and he ended up a rheumy-eyed old man in a tattered loincloth.

To a true Bedouin, such poverty hardly matters. Wealth—in the form of money, camels or other possessions—is most of all a medium for expressing lar-gess, something to be shared with companions of any description and with kinsmen in particular. As such it serves as part of a tribal welfare system.

There is an influential Rwala sheikh who is unstintingly generous to any kinsmen who are in need. When he has money, he strews it around like grass seed or he buys a new car—which two weeks later he usually gives away. As a result, he is sometimes so badly in need of funds that if his truck breaks down he has to borrow some money to have it fixed. He has no shame about doing so; in the Bedouin view, what flows out can be expected—Allah willing—to flow back in again. Although the continual giving of gifts may keep a man poor, it nevertheless serves as a mutual support

3

system that goes along with traditional tribal bonds.

Those bonds extend beyond the nomads to kin who have curtailed their migrations to raise sheep and goats, to those who have settled in villages, and even to those who are working in the oil fields, attending universities or employed in the cities.

When youths seek jobs in the oil fields and cities, they apply to firms where their kinsmen are already working. When they serve stints in the National Guard, they join units made up of kinsmen; a Western observer noted that some tents at a Saudi National Guard camp were overcrowded and others nearly empty because billeting was assigned by tribes. And when whole families elect to settle down, they do so among fellow tribesmen.

As the Bedouin turn away from the old way of life, one result has been the sprouting of new settlements. Typical of these is the village of Bushur, located in the Wadi Fatima, a river valley that runs between Mecca and Jidda. Bushur came into existence in 1953, when some families of the Harb tribe pitched their tents there to tend sheep and goats and raise crops.

At first glance, Bushur seems a transitory place, consisting of little more than some low adobe houses, some shacks made of palm fronds or flattened oil drums, and one or two tents.

As a member of the Royal Saudi National Guard, this Bedouin is able to maintain the warrior heritage of his people. The National Guard, which is directly controlled by the King as a counterbalance to the Saudi Arabian Army, is made up entirely of Bedouin.

But closer inspection reveals a pair of cement-lined wells, a number of homes built of concrete, three general shops and a small mosque–sure signs of an enduring settlement.

Several times a year, rains that fall in the surrounding mountains wash down through the wadi, leaving a deposit of silt and topsoil. By trapping the runoff in irrigation ditches and adding pump water from the wells, the villagers are able to raise two crops a year–usually melons in the summer, and in winter a variety of vegetables such as tomatoes, hot peppers and aubergines. Most of the households also maintain small flocks of sheep or goats, or both. No one has a camel, but some households keep donkeys for transportation and a few have bought trucks.

Despite these indications of a shift to a sedentary life, the old tribal patterns persist. Branches of the same tribe cluster their houses together. The houses themselves are divided within, like tents, into men's and women's sections. The same ceremonies of coffee drinking and lavish hospitality obtain. The village sheikh settles conflicts when they arise. Disputes usually concern such matters as well rights and pasturing rights. The penalty for the person deemed in the wrong is that he must slaughter a sheep and give a banquet for the aggrieved neighbour–just as would be the case in the desert.

All the same, villagers are making their way slowly into the modern world. They capitalize on their agriculture in a modest way by selling whatever they do not consume themselves. Each farmer employs two *jammals*–literally, "camelmen"–who nowadays drive trucks and take the farmer's produce to market in Mecca and Jidda. There the *jammal* turns the produce over to a food broker, who auctions it off and takes a 7.5 per cent commission on the prices the vegetables fetch. By comparison with the money that is to be made in the oil fields, the return to the farmer is minuscule–a mere $300 to $450 a year for most of the families, and virtually every family is in debt to the shopkeepers of their village.

Nevertheless, nearly all households have transistor radios on which they can tune in to *The Bedouin Hour*, a nightly programme that broadcasts mostly music, and many have sewing machines. There are several bicycles and even a motorcycle or two. The diet, already richer and more varied than desert fare, is also taking on a 20th-century cosmopolitan flavour. Youngsters in Bushur spurn dates and goat's milk for peanut-butter and jelly sandwiches–fare they have learnt to eat and like at school, where lunches are provided free for them.

Roughly half of the population is younger than 14; about 70 per cent of the boys between the ages of seven and 19 attend school in a neighbouring village, and more than half the girls are being tutored in Bushur itself. Most of the classes are at an elementary level, but several teenagers have moved on to high school, in the hope of eventually getting jobs that pay well.

After money, the greatest incentive to choose settlement among the peninsula's Bedouin is the promise of an education. Schools crop up everywhere. At one cluster of tents beside a well, a canvas tent 3 metres square serves as a schoolroom and as living quarters for the teacher. His meals are provided in the sheikh's tent–an instance of desert hospitality being adapted to the new order of things.

Every tribal elder, unlettered though he may be, has absorbed with his religion a near-reverence for book learning. According to a poll conducted by the Saudi government, even the Al Murrah, who of all tribes has resisted most the idea of settling down, is overwhelmingly in favour of sending the children to school. In some of the nomadic tribes, adults themselves take reading lessons from teachers whom the government sends to the nomads' summer encampments.

Most tribesmen are of two minds about the trends. They all hope for a better life, and even the most diehard camel herder dreams of land of his own where he can stop and shade himself under a stand of date palms when the spirit moves him. But he also wants to keep his camels and to preserve the sense of freedom and self-reliance that the desert gives him.

One sheikh explains it this way: "The oil wells can be blown up in 30 minutes and, with no money, all these people in Dhahran and Riyadh would die for lack of food. Why, they would not even have enough petrol to leave and go back to their homelands."

Equally compelling, perhaps, is simple nostalgia. A Western observer recalls an executive of an oil company interrupting a business meeting to talk wistfully about his family in the desert. "At this time, they will be here by the Well of the Old Camel," he said, pointing out a spot on a wall map that marked a well associated with tribal lore. "In another week or 10 days they will be at the Place of Lambing, 80 kilometres north." He moved his finger up the map. "Maybe I will see them in a month when they are here," he said with feeling. The desert is home and, for all the harshness of its way, it represents security of a kind.

From a rocky hilltop, a young Bedouin checks on the herd of female camels that supply his family with milk, a main element of their diet.

LIFE AMONG THE NOMADS

Although their lives are becoming increasingly modernized, the Bedouin have not abandoned the traditions born of their nomadic past. One of the hallmarks of their society is unstinting generosity to friends and strangers alike. And the preservation of bonds of kinship is all-important. The representatives of the Yam tribe seen here and on the following pages belong to three separate families, but they are linked by descent from a common ancestor five generations back. Most of the members of this group continue to wander with their herds of camels between the winter and summer grazing grounds, and wherever they go, they live close to one another.

Nonetheless, their lifestyle is changing in many ways. Instead of using their camels for transportation, they move about in pick-up trucks. They now send their children to school, and some of the men work in town to earn money to buy vehicles and other necessities. One family (*below*) has even built a permanent shelter for itself.

An elder confers with two women of his family in a hut strewn with bright rugs, while a baby sleeps nearby. Their corrugated zinc shelter is in the grazing area where the family customarily spends the winter.

Black-haired sheep rest under the blazing desert sun while children run a hose from a water tanker to fill a small trough for the animals. Such tankers enable the Bedouin to search for pasturage further from tribal wells than was the case in the past

Inside a spacious cloth tent from Pakistan, a veiled woman reclines against a small chest. Tents like this and the white canvas variety seen on the right are increasingly common because Bedouin women no longer weave their own goat-hair tents.

Controlling his horse with only a
halter, a youth rides bareback into the
desert. Many Bedouin remain skilful
horsemen, but the swift Arab steeds,
formerly used for intertribal raiding,
now serve primarily as status symbols.

A diligent youngster practises writing
as his proud family looks on. The boy
commutes to school, leaving every
morning at 5.30 for the 19-kilometre
truck journey out to a paved road to
catch the school bus.

Three Bedouin men feast on a special meal of goat meat, rice, cheese and dates. The Bedouin eat meat only rarely, but—as is the case here—they will slaughter a goat to honour their guests. Following Arabian custom, all use only the right hand for eating from the communal platter.

A Bedouin host pounds roasted coffee beans in a brass mortar. The blackened kettle on the right is for boiling water, the many gracefully shaped brass pots for serving the coffee.

After eating, a guest unwinds his headdress to allow the incense contained in the studded brass burner to perfume his hair and beard.

83

A Bedouin elder whose family keeps a
small herd of camels tries to get a stud
camel to sit down. The camel is
tethered to a thorn-bush in order to
keep it from wandering.

While the Bedouin milks a camel from one side, squeezing the fluid into a bowl, a calf nurses on the other side, stimulating the mother's flow.

Burying his nose in white foam, the elder drinks deeply of camel's milk. As well as being a dietary staple, the milk is always offered to guests as part of the ritual of Bedouin hospitality.

Flanked by her daughters and
daughter-in-law on the women's side
of the family tent, a matriarch spins
wool that she will later use to weave a
tent divider like the one seen here.

Grimacing with the effort, a woman
shakes a heavy goatskin bag full of
goat's milk to make thin, clarified
butter for her family; the churning
will take her about an hour.

While her menfolk prostrate themselves in prayer, a young woman tends a child and stirs roasting coffee beans; according to custom, the woman will worship separately.

Through these pipes, oil surges from storage tanks on Kuwait's coast to tankers waiting offshore. Kuwait is the world's richest country in terms of gross national product per capita ($20,079 in 1980 versus $11,360 for the U.S.), and more than 92 per cent of its revenues come from petroleum.

BURIED TREASURE
IN HILLS OF SAND

In terms of potential impact, few royal decisions in history have been so thoroughly underestimated as King Abd al-Aziz ibn Saud's agreement in 1933 to grant an American oil company the right to extract petroleum from his desert in return for a couple of chestfuls of gold coins. The oil was to make Saudi Arabia and the neighbouring sheikhdoms on the Arabian Gulf the richest and fastest-changing societies in the modern world. It would also, not incidentally, give them a major role to play in international affairs.

The concession agreement delighted the King—not because he had any real sense of the wealth and power that lay in the future, but for more immediate reasons. The Great Depression had severely straitened the royal exchequer; its principal source of revenue was the tax (the equivalent of about $250 per person) paid by foreigners who undertook the annual religious pilgrimage to Mecca, and their numbers had decreased dramatically, from 132,000 in 1927 to only 38,500 in 1931. That represented a loss of more than $23 million, and the kingdom was sorely in debt to private bankers and to friendly governments that had lent it money.

In granting the oil concession, Ibn Saud had nothing to lose. He strongly suspected that the sands of his barren land concealed only worthless rock. At best, the geologists might find fresh water, the peninsula's most basic need.

As all the world knows with hindsight, the sub-surface rock Ibn Saud thought was worthless turned out to contain both water and oil in prodigious quantities. Indeed, the eastern portion of the Arabian Peninsula, which is covered by a relatively thin layer of sedimentary rocks, harbours most of the world's known reserves of oil and gas. It is part of what is known as the Arabian Shelf, which stretches under the Rub'al-Khali and the Gulf into Bahrain and Iran.

Some 550 million years ago, a sea covered the entire area. The waters teemed with marine life, which died and drifted to the ocean floor in a steady organic rain. There the remains decomposed among mineral salts in the mud and sand. In cycles of 100 million years or more, the sea ebbed and flowed, exposing its floor to the forces of sun and wind when it receded and laying down a new layer of sediments when it returned. In the process, the combined sediments began to form the stratified limestone and sandstone of today's Arabian Shelf.

After the shelf had accumulated several layers, tectonic movements in the earth's crust caused it to buckle and fold, forcing the uppermost layers into mounds and ridges known as domes and anticlines. In some areas the movements produced outcroppings of rock that were later sculpted by erosion. In other areas they buried the new layers.

4

In still others they created fissures. Deep in the subterranean interstices of all that folded, buckled and rippled mass, some of the decomposed marine life began to change into gas and oil.

In the aeons while this was occurring, changes in climatic conditions were affecting the earth from above. Towards the end of the ice ages, the glaciers that covered much of the Northern Hemisphere began retreating; southern monsoonal rains now shifted northwards, drenching the Arabian Peninsula and greening it. The excess rainfall seeped into the creviced and porous limestone of the Arabian Shelf and accumulated there, with the marine life metamorphosing into oil.

Some of these primordial accumulations of oil and water were buried as much as 4 or 5 kilometres beneath the surface and lay there undetected until recent times. But not all of them. The oasis springs from which the Arabians drank and watered their animals and crops came from underground supplies of water known as aquifers; some of these springs flowed liberally on the surface, while others ran close enough to the surface for hand-wielded picks and shovels to reach.

Similarly, some of the oil oozed out at the surface, and some of the gas escaped. The "pitch" with which Noah caulked his ark would have been petroleum that had seeped out of the earth. Such free-flowing petroleum was used also by other ancient residents of the Middle East to fuel their lamps and to make mortar for their buildings.

Gas had no known uses, although Arabs in Mesopotamia wrote in the ninth century A.D. of "eternal fires" that they deemed to be magic. Modern geologists know that such fires result when natural gas has been ignited by lightning or by man-made sparks; once lit, they will continue to burn as long as gas continues to feed the flame.

Not until late in the 19th century did Western engineers discover that oil was the ideal fuel for running machinery. At that point, they began to search for oil with a sense of urgency. The Middle East was the logical place to look, and soon the area was crawling with prospectors. The British found oil in Iran as early as 1908 and in Iraq in 1927.

In 1928 an American-owned firm, the Standard Oil Company of California, known acronymically as Socal, acquired a concession on the Gulf island of Bahrain. Nearly four years were to go by before drilling got under way. Meanwhile, Socal officials had been casting covetous eyes across the water that separated Bahrain from the peninsula, where a series of hills looked temptingly like oil-bearing formations. But the American oilmen were unable to approach King Ibn Saud, who kept a wary distance from foreigners. "My kingdom will survive only insofar as it remains a country of difficult access," he was later to say. Unbeknownst to himself or to the Socal officials, however, a cast of colourful characters was paving the way for the oil company's entry into Saudi Arabia.

Among these was a 73-year-old American millionaire, Charles R. Crane, heir to a family fortune made from manufacturing baths, sinks and toilets. Crane himself, a do-gooder by nature, had left the plumbing business in 1914 for a career of part-time diplomacy and full-time philanthropy. A stint as co-chairman of a special commission named by President Woodrow Wilson to investigate Palestine in the aftermath of World War I left him a self-styled "friend of the Arabs". At his own expense, he undertook to finance the education of young Arabs abroad, and in 1927 he sent a team of engineers to Yemen to construct windmills for pumping water.

Crane had tried twice during the 1920s to see Ibn Saud—with no better luck than the representatives of Socal. The King had no idea why Crane wanted to meet him; besides, he was too busy to spare the time. On one occasion, Crane made it to the Red Sea port of Jidda and left behind with one of Saud's ministers a sample of the family company's workmanship, a four-footed pink enamel bath. Because Saudi Arabia had no water system to which it could be connected, the bath thereafter occupied a place of honour on the roof of the minister's palace—but it did nothing to advance Crane's cause.

Crane was persistent, however, and the King finally agreed to meet him in Jidda. Indeed, he not only met Crane but, true to his reputation as a desert host, received him royally with a banquet of whole boiled sheep, and had his guards and retinue perform the *ardha*, a ceremonial war dance. He presented Crane with a pair of magnificent stallions—and magnanimously refrained from any show of disdain when Crane reciprocated with a box of California dates grown on his own estate.

Crane had, of course, largess of a more substantial sort at his command. When the King expressed an interest in finding new sources of water, Crane obliged with a promise to supply an expert surveyor, among other things. Soon thereafter he sent the King a list of names, from which Ibn Saud chose one at random—Karl Twitchell.

Twitchell was a mining engineer from Vermont. When Crane asked him to come to Saudi Arabia in April 1931, he was already in Yemen, building foundations for a steel-truss road bridge to cross a large wadi. He readily agreed to search for water, and Ibn Saud took an instant liking to him.

During the next year, Twitchell made several long expeditions up and down the Saudi desert, but he had no success. Hearing that oil had been struck on Bahrain, however, Twitchell passed the news to the King. "There is little difference in geology between Bahrain and the mainland," he told Ibn Saud, "so if oil was found there you would probably have it in your country." Interested, Ibn Saud com-missioned Twitchell to communicate to American oil companies that he was now willing to discuss granting conces-sions to look for oil in Saudi Arabia. Here was a way to raise the money he badly needed.

Twitchell approached Socal, which had investigated every possible means of reaching Ibn Saud. The company was delighted to co-operate and al-ready had a man picked out to nego-tiate with the King on Socal's behalf. This was Harry St. John Philby, a 47-year-old Englishman educated at Cambridge who was an even more de-dicated Arabophile than Crane and Twitchell. Philby had served as a Bri-tish colonial officer in India, Mesopo-tamia and Transjordan. Fed up with the British Colonial Service, he retired in 1925 and settled in Jidda, where he made a living selling Arabians such Western marvels as Model A Fords, Marconi radio sets and Lever Brothers Sunlight soap.

Philby was a bundle of contradic-tions. He remained staunchly British in manner and outlook, yet he tried to be as Arabian as he could. He dressed in Arab *thawb* and *ghutra*. He even dared to cross the forbidding Rub'al-Khali, a feat that took him three months and the

OIL'S UNDERGROUND HIDING PLACES

Oil fills deep subterranean pools along the eastern portion of the Arabian Peninsula and under the Arabian Gulf, as this map of the area's proven oil reserves shows. The greatest concentration occurs within Saudi Arabia. The kingdom has not only the world's largest reserves of oil, but its largest field—Ghawar, 240 kilometres long and 40 kilometres wide. Some of Saudi Arabia's oil still flows through Ras Tanura, from which it was first shipped 50 years ago.

help of 14 Bedouin and 32 camels, and earned him international celebrity. Although he had been an avowed atheist, he embraced Islam. His conversion scandalized Englishmen, but it gave him access to Ibn Saud's inner circle, where he became a confidant and adviser to the King.

In the lavish manner of the desert host, King Ibn Saud bestowed on Philby a house in Mecca, his own slave girl and a Muslim name–Abdallah, "Slave of God". Cynical Jidda merchants huffed that the name should have been Abd al-Qirsh, "Slave of sixpence", since they could only assume that the Englishman's motive for converting to Islam was self-gain.

In May 1932, Philby was in London on a speaking tour following his successful crossing of the Rub'al-Khali, and it was there that Socal's representative approached him with the idea of seeking an oil concession from Ibn Saud. Philby agreed to do so. Returning to Saudi Arabia with a secret monthly retainer of $1,000 to advance the oil company's interests, he participated in the negotiations between Socal and the King's representatives in Jidda that took place in February of 1933. Twitchell was also present, as a technical adviser to Socal and as the only person who had examined the terrain with a geologist's eye.

The King was a tough bargainer. He

wanted a down payment in gold that amounted to about 100,000 pounds, and Socal offered him no more than half of that to start. Moreover, Socal wanted to pay the major part of its fee in the form of future royalties, and the King wanted cash at once.

After three months of painstaking negotiation in which Philby served as go-between, Socal representatives and the King's finance minister, Abdallah al-Sulaiman, reached a compromise. The final agreement, worked out in British pounds because British currency was the one honoured throughout the Middle East, stipulated that the oil company would pay King Ibn Saud £30,000 as a down payment and then £5,000 per year in rent. It included a promise of an additional £20,000 after 18 months and £50,000 more if and when oil should be discovered. All this was an advance against royalties of 4 shillings per ton once oil was extracted from the ground. In exchange, Socal was granted the exclusive right to prospect for and produce oil for 60 years in Saudi Arabia's Eastern Province, a 930,000-square-kilometre area of the Gulf coast.

. The advance payment of £30,000 and the first year's £5,000 rent amounted to only 35 per cent of the King's initial demand, and it would one day be applied towards royalties. Nevertheless, the King had for all practical purposes got what he wanted. With the subsequent installments, he was guaranteed a sum total of £55,000 for the first year and a half, and he would be able to keep that money even if never a drop of oil turned up.

In May 1933, the group of negotiators met to present the agreement to the King. As his finance minister read the long and complicated terms aloud, Ibn Saud dozed off. Then he woke with a start and asked the advice of Philby, who assured him that it was the best he could get. "Very well," the King told his finance minister. "Put your trust in God and sign."

It took a great deal of trust to sustain all concerned, for the historic agreement was no sooner signed than the first of several snags developed. Even though he had yielded on the figure, the King still wanted his down payment in gold; but U.S. President Franklin D. Roosevelt had just imposed an embargo on the export of gold in order to avert a brewing panic over Depression bank failures. Another three months were to elapse during which time Socal discreetly bought the gold in London and shipped it by steamer to Jidda.

Eventually, on August 25, Twitchell counted out 35,000 gold sovereigns under the watchful eye of Finance Minister al-Sulaiman. It is a measure of the kingdom's fiduciary practices that Su-

Geologist Max Steineke, who was most responsible for completing Saudi Arabia's first successful oil well in 1938, cleaves a rock sample with a hammer. Admiring Saudis called him a "big man with a big arm and a big voice". By 1985 the well had produced more than 32 million barrels.

laiman's sons remember seeing the gold arrive at their home in chests in the summer of 1933.

Socal wasted no further time in proceeding with the search for oil. It created a wholly owned subsidiary called Casoc (another acronym, this one standing for California-Arabian Standard Oil Company) and sent a team of geologists to the coastal village of Damma, just across the Arabian Gulf from the island of Bahrain.

The geologists had a tough time. The area was so utterly remote from civilization that they had to take with them—by truck and camel caravan—everything they needed, from girders and drill bits to toilets, fans and electric wiring. They had to set about founding a community and searching for oil in a region known for its fierce sandstorms and heat that often climbed to about 50°C by midday. Furthermore, although the oil-bearing formations were definitely there, they did not reveal themselves readily. Percolating ground water had dissolved the underlying rock, causing the formations to slump, and wind-blown mounds of sand had obscured them even more.

Ibn Saud provided Bedouin guides to help the geologists find their way about the desert, but the Bedouin frustrated their employers by stopping five times daily for prayers. The guides, in turn, were baffled by the geologists. Once the King paid a visit to the camp and asked the chief guide how the Casoc men were going about their work. "May God prolong your life, the thing they mostly pick up, the thing they look for most, is anything that shows the mark of the sea," the guide replied. "I, by God, do not know the reason for their aim at all."

After 18 months of surveying on foot,

4

by truck and by plane, the geologists still had little more to go by than the hills that had already been spotted from Bahrain. So at length they decided to pick an area located just inland from their field camp near Dammam. They named it the Dammam Dome and started drilling at a village by the name of Dhahran in April 1935.

Now began a three-year phase of repeated frustrations. The oilmen drilled one well after another, 10 in all, some of them below the 1,000-metre depth at which oil had been found on Bahrain. To the delight of Ibn Saud, the drillers' bits struck water—but to the geologists' disappointment, very little oil. Socal poured so much money into drilling that, in the autumn of 1936, to gain new capital, it sold half-ownership in the concession to Texaco, the Texas Oil Company, for $21 million.

As the year 1936 drew to a close, the Socal authorities in California were almost at the point of giving up on the fledgling company. But their chief geologist, Max Steineke, was confident that there was oil in the region, and he persuaded them to let him keep going with the search.

Steineke decided to stake everything on one final effort. He ordered further drilling at the well that seemed to him to be the most promising, No. 7. Still there was no sign of any oil, and everything possible went wrong, including cave-ins, stuck drill bits and even an explosion of natural gas that sent the entire assemblage of rigging and drill soaring into the air.

Then, on March 4, 1938, at a depth of 1,440 metres, Steineke got his reward—and the company's—when oil began to flow from a thick seam of porous limestone. The more that the men drilled, the more they found; in three

Guided by an American oilman in Arab dress *(below, right)*, King Abd al-Aziz ibn Saud makes his first tour of a drilling platform in 1939. Impressed by the visit, the King extended the area leased to Casoc, the firm then jointly backed by two American oil companies.

weeks the oil was flowing at the prodigious rate of 3,810 barrels a day.

Now ready to go into business at last, the engineers built a 70-kilometre, 25-centimetre pipeline north from the Dammam field to the village of Ras Tanura on the coast, where they also built a port to handle ocean-going tankers. In the spring of 1939 the first one arrived to carry the Saudi crude oil out of the Gulf, around the peninsula, up the Red Sea, and through the Suez Canal to the Mediterranean and the West. When, on May 1 of that year, King Ibn Saud turned the valve through which his newfound wealth would flow into the tanker, Saudi Arabia was on the threshold of a new age.

So were the other countries of the region. Bahrain, which had been steadily pumping since 1932, was now also the site of a refinery. Oil had been found in Kuwait as well, and Qatar seemed another promising area.

The dividends were delayed, however, because the sudden flow of oil in the Arabian Peninsula coincided with the outbreak of World War II in 1939. Large-scale production had hardly begun before it was suspended. German and Italian submarines and planes made the route through the Mediterranean too dangerous.

After the war, production not only quickly accelerated, but also expanded beyond the wildest dreams of the oilmen. New geophysical techniques made it possible for geologists to locate additional oil fields. And demand in the West kept pace with supply as cars for family use proliferated, together with aeroplanes for public transport and tractors for farm work. Oil generated the electricity that in turn provided the power for everything from giant industrial turbines to the toasters on kitchen tables all over the world.

But in the economic and technological explosion that attended the postwar recovery, machinery was no longer the sole impetus for exploiting oil. Its unprecedented abundance gave rise to entire new industries based on oil derivatives—plastics, chemical fertilizers, synthetic fabrics and detergents. All these developments together brought a tenfold jump in the demand for oil in the two decades that followed the end of World War II.

To exploit the finds and satisfy the rising demand for oil required vast amounts of new capital. The California Standard and Texas Oil Companies therefore sought new partners. In 1948 Standard Oil of New York (then called

A rig drives its drill through the sands of the Rub'al-Khali, Saudi Arabia's France-sized desert area. Once empty except for nomadic Bedouin and their camels, the Rub'al-Khali has become pockmarked with oil-drilling outposts.

Socony-Vacuum, later Mobil) and Standard Oil of New Jersey (later known as Esso and subsequently as Exxon) joined the undertaking, which by then had been renamed Aramco, for Arabian American Oil Company.

Already oil production had soared from 21 million barrels a year at war's end to 143 million barrels in 1948, and it was increasing at an annual rate of almost 19 per cent. Not surprisingly, the thought had begun to dawn in many an Arab mind that the nation yielding the oil was entitled to a bigger share in the profits than the agreements stipulated.

Accordingly, the original concession that Saudi Arabia had negotiated with Socal in 1933 was renegotiated with Aramco in 1950, and the profits on the sale of a barrel of crude oil were thence-

forth to be divided equally between Saudi Arabia and the oil company. Other concessionaries and their host countries followed suit, and the 50-50 arrangement soon prevailed throughout the Gulf region.

The arrangement benefited all concerned. In the first year alone, it nearly doubled Ibn Saud's revenues, from $56.7 million to $110 million. The oil companies for the first time were able to write off as income tax their payments to the host governments and then deduct the payments from taxable income at home.

In the heady days of the 1950s, even the consumers benefited. Average daily production of crude oil throughout the Middle East went to about 500,000 barrels in 1950 and doubled by 1958.

As production went up, the cost of producing went down–and so did prices to the consumer. Oil of a quality that had sold for $2.80 per barrel in 1948 dropped to $1.80 per barrel in 1960. In the context of inflation, which was causing the price of everything else in the West to rise, oil was one of the bargains of the decade.

The pricing was an arcane process determined by the foreign oil companies that controlled the concessions throughout the Middle East. By now these companies included Socal, Esso, Texaco and Mobil (the four parent companies of Aramco) in Saudi Arabia; Gulf Oil in Kuwait; British Petroleum in Kuwait, Iraq and Iran; and Royal Dutch Shell in Iraq, Iran and Oman. A few other oil companies were now oper-

ating in the Middle East, but the Seven Sisters, as the major corporations were called, settled prices in conjunction with one another—and in blithe disregard of the host countries whose oil they drew.

Because production continued to increase, the producing countries grew richer. Towards the end of the decade, however, they began to perceive that their share in the profits was diminishing. The 50-50 arrangement by which the oil companies ostensibly split the profits with them was calculated after expenses. But the oil company books—and thus the evidence of how their expenses had been computed—were closed to the host countries. One indignant Saudi—Abdallah Tariki, who was Director-General of Petro-

leum in the Ministry of Finance—estimated that the alleged 50-50 split of the profits actually worked out to 68-32, with the Saudi Arabians being on the short end of the bargain.

Whatever share the host countries were receiving, they were getting it only on the profits from the sale of crude oil. The oil companies, on the other hand, kept an iron grip on refining, shipping and marketing, increasing their profits exponentially.

It took two very small and seemingly innocuous price cuts on the part of the oil companies to provoke the oil-producing countries to action. In the August of 1960, the Seven Sisters summarily lowered the price of oil by 10 cents a barrel—for the second time in 10 months. Those few cents boded a

loss of $30 million in profits for Saudi Arabia alone in the coming year. To make matters worse, Saudi Arabia had not only had no say in the matter, but also was taken by surprise; and the price reduction jeopardized a budget that Crown Prince Faisal had painstakingly worked out for the coming year.

Now Tariki was not the only indignant Arabian. With Faisal's blessing, Tariki rounded up representatives of Iran, Iraq, Kuwait and Venezuela, the four countries that together with Saudi Arabia produced 80 per cent of the world's supply of oil. On September 9, 1960, they announced the creation of the Organization of Petroleum Exporting Countries. They issued a declaration demanding that the oil companies maintain stable prices, and they

Because oil is almost always out of sight in pipes, this leak in a buried pipeline offers a rare glimpse of the liquid that has made the Arabian Peninsula rich. Oil leaks are rare, and instruments quickly detect any drop in pipeline pressure.

pledged their countries to stick together in pressing that demand.

OPEC, as the group would later be known, had taken a fateful step towards claiming control of the precious oil that its members supplied and the rest of the world had come to depend on. But as yet it had no machinery for enforcing its demands, and for more than a decade it remained an organization with no significant power. "We don't recognize this so-called OPEC," declared Bob Brougham, President of Aramco. "Our dealings are with Saudi Arabia, not with outsiders."

However, with unruffled determination, Ahmad Saki Yamani, a Mecca-born, Harvard-educated lawyer who took over as Saudi Arabia's oil minister, began speaking in 1968 of "participation downstream," by which he meant that the oil-producing countries should share in the profits of refining, shipping and marketing. The oil companies paid no heed.

The turning point for OPEC came in October 1973, when Egypt went to war against Israel and suddenly oil became a political weapon of unexpected clout.

The war broke out just as OPEC and the heads of the oil companies were convening in Vienna. There, the oil-producing countries proposed raising the price of a barrel of oil, then about three dollars, to slightly over five dollars. The oil companies countered with a skimpy 15 per cent offer. When the oil producers held fast and repeated their demand for a two-dollar price increase, the oil companies argued that such an enormous jump would have far-reaching effects on the world economy; they asked for two weeks to consult with their governments.

Before the two weeks had elapsed, the United States had announced a

In a complex of towers and pipes, an Abu Dhabi plant uses refrigeration to condense natural gas into a liquid form for shipping. By the early 1980s the United Arab Emirates, including Abu Dhabi, annually produced 2.2 million tonnes of liquefied natural gas.

massive appropriation of $2.2 billion in aid to Israel. Nothing could have infuriated the oil-producing countries more. As Arabs, they naturally sided with Egypt, whether or not they were participating actively in the war. For the United States–or any other nation that depended on Middle Eastern oil–to side with Israel seemed to the Arab nations insulting.

They expressed their outrage by slapping an embargo on oil shipments to all nations that supported Israel. The result was an oil panic all over the world. In the United States, great queues formed at petrol stations, thermostats were turned down in private homes and public buildings, and national monuments that had formerly been lit by night suddenly went dark.

By December, foreign ministers and other highly placed diplomats from Japan, France, Belgium, Germany, Italy, Switzerland and Greece were trooping to the Middle Eastern capitals to plead for oil; the U.S. honoured Saudi Arabia with the first visit by a Secretary of

State in 20 years; and the British Trade Secretary and the Chancellor of the Exchequer ambushed the Shah of Iran on the ski slopes of St. Moritz to barter £100 million of British goods for five million tons of oil.

Now the five-dollar price that the oil companies had spurned in October began to look like a bargain; by the new year, the prevailing price for oil was $11.25 a barrel, and some of the supplicants for oil paid as much as $17. "We have you–how you say it?–over a barrel," one OPEC representative would point out to an oilman. From there the price was to climb further in the coming months. Meanwhile, prices on stock exchanges all over the world fell precipitously, and London's *Financial Times* observed wryly: "The future will be subject to delay."

For the Arabian Peninsula, on the contrary, the future was to happen with overwhelming speed. Never again would the oil-producing countries have to plead to be included in pricing; they now had the deciding voice in that and

A farm family rides a donkey cart along a paved road that runs parallel to one of the broad, modern canals in Saudi Arabia's largest oasis, Al-Hasa. Using oil money, the government has rebuilt virtually the entire Al-Hasa water system since the 1960s.

other matters as well. In March of 1974, in exchange for a promise of U.S. help in expediting a stoppage of the war, OPEC lifted the embargo. Only then did oil resume its flow to the West.

Meanwhile, negotiations for "participation" went forward. By the end of 1974, Saudi Arabia owned a 60 per cent share of Aramco and in 1980 the Saudi government obtained 100 per cent of the company's assets. One by one the other nations took over their concessions–gradually and peaceably. "The colonial era is gone forever," said Yamani. "We are masters of our own affairs, and we will decide what to do with our oil."

Today the governments of the Arabian Peninsula are masters of an immense petroleum-producing complex that includes hundreds of wells. They have gained control of all aspects of oil production, including refining and transportation to storage tanks. In addition, they control reserves amounting to hundreds of billions of barrels still untouched a kilometre or more below ground. Geologists today believe that oil lies under almost the entire length of the peninsula.

Of the crude oil produced, about one third goes to the peninsula's more than a dozen refineries for cracking into petrol, diesel fuel and other finished products, most of which are for domestic consumption. The rest of the crude is piped to 15 ports on the Arabian Peninsula for export. Ras Tanura, where the lone tanker carried away the historic first shipment of Saudi crude in 1939, has in recent years dispatched more than 3,000 tankers a year. Loaded supertankers, departing from other ports every day of the week, have carried up to nine million barrels daily. In addition to all that, the oil-producing states

have begun to make profits on the natural gases that are found in the earth together with oil.

The gases have represented an unexpected bonanza. Until the price of oil soared during the 1970s, they were considered a nuisance and more often than not were burnt off at the oil fields. But with the development of means of liquefying the gases through supercooling, it has become possible to transport the fuel to distant markets. The resulting liquid propane and butane provide power for any number of embryonic industries on the peninsula, and there is still enough left over to be exported.

Oil production no longer goes up automatically and irrevocably; in 1976 Kuwait set a precedent by severely cutting back on its production in order to conserve its reserves. That step reflects

At Qidah, an Omani seacoast village favoured with its own fresh-water well, workers use a hose to fill water tanks on a boat. The craft will deliver its cargo to nearby communities with inadequate supplies of potable water.

a dilemma that the Arabian countries were obliged to confront once they had taken control of their oil. As an oil expert in Qatar put it, "A barrel sold is a barrel lost."

Had the production rate prevailing on the eve of the 1973 crisis continued unchecked, the reserves would have been exhausted in less than a hundred years, according to one reckoning. To retain and build upon the enormous wealth that oil has brought them, the Arabian states must achieve a balance between present needs (their own revenues, as well as fuel for the industrialized nations of the world) and the needs of generations yet to be born.

Meanwhile, the oil boom has made great demands on that historically scarcest of natural resources–water. To sustain the increasingly urbanized societies that oil has brought, the Arabs require increasing supplies of fresh water–for agriculture, for hygiene and for drinking. In the early 1980s, petrol could be had in Riyadh for 18 cents per 4 litres; the same amount of bottled drinking water cost $2.40–and that is just one reflection of the scarcity of water in this riverless and nearly rainless part of the world.

Quite apart from its scarcity, rainfall on the peninsula presents special problems. On parts of the Gulf coast, where the rainfall averages about 10 centimetres a year, virtually all of it comes down in one or two fierce storms. One storm in Sharjah in the United Arab Emirates released 10 centimetres in just 24 hours. The runoff from such a deluge may course down a wadi and build into a wall of water so high that people actually drown in the desert. In the Asir highlands of southern Saudi Arabia and in the mountainous reaches of northern Yemen, where the Indian

Ocean monsoons send more bountiful rains of 50 centimetres a year, the rush of water erodes the topsoil. Some of this water seeps into the ground, but most of it simply evaporates.

Long before the dawn of history, farmers of the peninsula learnt to turn the circumstances that nature gave them to their own advantage. In the Asir and Yemen they terraced the hillsides with low fieldstone walls, slowing the runoff, retarding erosion and trapping moisture. Across the wadis they constructed dams and lined them with stone to trap the rainfall. When needed, the water was diverted through a network of ditches to the fields. Such systems are still used today.

By custom that goes back more centuries than anyone can remember, the dams are opened for the farmers in turn, starting at the upper reaches of the hillsides. Each farmer is permitted to fill his plot until the water is ankle-deep. Then the sluice to his field is closed off and another one is opened to send the water flowing onto the next terrace below.

On the opposite side of the peninsula, where Oman's mountains peter out into the lowlands of the Rub'al-Khali and the deserts of the United Arab Emirates, the people get water by means of hand-dug underground conduits called *aflaj*. The idea for this irrigation system came from Persia more than a thousand years ago. *Aflaj* are still in use today. At Al Ayn in the Buraimi Oasis in the United Arab Emirates, 41 million litres a day flow through a network of 16 tunnels. The Omani people still include in their ritual greeting an inquiry as to the state of the *aflaj*. The respectful answer to give is, "May they be full."

In actual fact, not all of the *aflaj* on the peninsula are full, for in recent years the older canals have fallen into disrepair. Of the more than 80 *aflaj* known to exist in the United Arab Emirates, only 25 were usable at the start of the 1980s because the proliferation of industry and the growth of cities had overtaxed them. Some of them had become clogged with sand while others had been abandoned because the water table had subsided.

Luckily for the people everywhere on the peninsula, the oilmen with their powerful drilling rigs have uncovered water resources the Arabians did not even know they had. Geologists have discovered that aquifers underlie two

4

thirds of the peninsula, even the vast wasteland of the Rub'al-Khali. Some of them cover several hundred thousand square kilometres.

The aquifers are the legacy of the long-vanished rainfalls that occurred during epochs when the peninsula was green. They were aeons in forming; laboratory analysis shows that the water in some of them has been there for 20,000 to 40,000 years.

Today, tapping aquifers is big business. Because it comes from limestone and sandstone, most aquifer water contains high concentrations of minerals and salts and must be treated to be fit for human consumption. The fast-growing city of Riyadh, where the population rose from 350,000 in 1970 to more than a million residents by 1980, depends for its life on the purified water of three different aquifers, one of which is 450 kilometres away and 1,280 metres below the surface.

Even the Arabian Peninsula's largest and oldest oasis—al-Hasa, which is blessed with a profusion of 162 natural springs—needs the assistance of modern engineering in order to make the best use of its water. In the mid-1960s the government of Saudi Arabia found that the region's once-adequate agriculture was falling on hard times. Investigating the matter, government agents discovered that the troubles ranged from antiquated customs to over-enthusiastic water consumption.

Since time out of mind, custom had differentiated between two kinds of irrigation water. The first was *hurr*, water that flowed directly from a spring to a settler's garden. The second was *tawayih*, water that had run off from gardens irrigated with *hurr*.

Because the one was presumably a gift from Allah and the other the hand-

MAKING THE DESERT BLOOM

Lettuce thrives in an experimental greenhouse 80 kilometres outside Riyadh.

Water—or the lack of it—has always been the major constraint on agriculture in the Arabian Peninsula, and in some ways oil money has exacerbated the problem. With increased urbanization and rising incomes, people's tastes and expectations changed. In Saudi Arabia, farm workers dropped from 40 per cent of the labour force in the mid-1970s to less than 25 per cent in the early 1980s.

Not surprisingly, the once self-sufficient peninsula has grown ever more dependent on food imports. The only country whose imports account for less than half its domestic consumption is South Yemen—the rain-blessed Arabia Felix of old. In Saudi Arabia, where less than 1 per cent of the land is under cultivation, food imports constitute 80 per cent of domestic consumption.

For nearly two decades, the Saudi government has sought to reverse

the trend, with some success. It has provided incentives to boost private-sector investment in agriculture. By investing capital directly in dam construction and irrigation projects, it has helped to control flash floods and make water available for use in fields—with the result that thousands of hectares of once arid land are now productive. It has also subsidized the increased planting of certain crops. Indeed, subsidies to encourage the production of wheat were so successful that between 1979 and 1981 the ratio of locally grown wheat to total domestic wheat consumption rose from 3.6 to 27.8 per cent.

The government also runs more than a dozen model farms and experimental research stations. In huge greenhouses like the one above, agricultural planners have tested high-yield seeds and hydroponic growing methods to find ways to make the desert bloom.

me-down of fellow humans, the owners of gardens watered by *hurr* automatically had greater prominence in the social structure of the oasis than those consigned to *tawayih*. Thus a farmer who enjoyed *hurr* water was expected to provide the same benefit for each of his sons. To make this possible, every farmer lucky enough to have *hurr* water dug more and more canals from the springs. The proliferation of canals led to greater water loss through evaporation and through seepage into the ground, and in its passage from one field to the other, the water soaked up more and more salt from the ground. By the time it reached the edge of the oasis, it was so salty that gardens there began dying out.

Worst of all was the arrival in al-Hasa of modern plumbing, which used up a prodigal 7,500 litres of water per capita per day. Accustomed as they were to aridity, the citizens of al-Hasa squandered the water with abandon when they suddenly had it easily available in their households. The mere sight and sound of clear, cool water was such an enormous source of psychological satisfaction that they simply hated to turn off their taps.

To revive al-Hasa agriculture, the Saudi government embarked upon a massive reconstruction of the irrigation system in 1965. A force of 3,000 men laboured for more than seven years, tapping several aquifers and constructing a new 1,500-kilometre water-distribution system. They also built an equally extensive drainage network to divert the used saline water away from the oasis. To satisfy the people's need to have their water constantly in view, the engineers kept it visible in open canals instead of burying it in pipelines. This new system has proved to be

so efficient–and complex–that all distinctions between *hurr* and *tawayih* have vanished. Now in al-Hasa all water is the same, and it is put to better use than ever in the fields.

By the 1980s, agriculture at the oasis had made a comeback. A total of more than 12,000 hectares of cultivated land supported a population of nearly 400,000 inhabitants in dozens of towns and villages. Rich alfalfa fields provided sustenance for animals, and no fewer than three million date palms were producing not only fruit for local consumption, but also a surplus that would be sold elsewhere.

Al-Hasa has proved to be an object lesson for Arabians everywhere. Throughout the peninsula, steps are being taken to ensure that there will be adequate supplies of fresh water in the future. In 1980 the Kingdom of Saudi Arabia earmarked $12 billion from its oil revenues for various means of obtaining water. Plans call for building 37 new dams to impound rainfall and for constructing treatment plants where urban waste water can be recycled. Saudi government officials predict that by the year 2000 some 15 per cent of the kingdom's water will be derived from reclamation plants.

A jump ahead of Saudi Arabia was the sheikhdom of Kuwait, which used to import thousands of litres of water from Iraq (the water was carried in goatskins). In 1953 Kuwait built the area's first desalination plant, which distilled fresh water from the sea by an intricate condensation process.

By 1980, Kuwait's desalination plants were daily furnishing nearly 400 million litres of potable water–75 per cent of the state's needs–and other countries had followed Kuwait's lead. Abu Dhabi of the United Arab Emir-

ates is largely dependent on desalination for its potable water. Desalination now provides much of the potable water in all the oil-producing countries of the peninsula.

Arabians relentlessly explore other possibilities. The most visionary proposal originated with a maverick of the royal house of Saudi Arabia. In 1977 Prince Muhammad ibn Faisal, former director of the kingdom's desalination programme, formed a company to investigate the possibility of making use of Antarctica's mammoth icebergs. What the Prince specifically had in mind involved towing a 90-million-tonne berg 14,000 kilometres from Antarctic waters to the Red Sea port of Jidda. There it would be melted to release the enormous quantities of fresh water locked up in its bulk.

When it cost the Prince one million dollars just to gather information, he realized that this enticing idea entails a multitude of problems. No one has yet engineered a vessel powerful enough to tow an iceberg of that size from Antarctica, or a means of insulation to keep the berg from breaking up and melting en route, or even an efficient way to get the water from the berg on arrival. Stymied by the technical complexities, the Prince decided to suspend work on the project in 1981.

Meanwhile, the discovery and availability of ever deeper aquifers (which became feasible as improvements in drilling technology proceeded hand in hand with rising oil production) and an increased use of desalination (made possible through electric-powered machinery) have indirectly fulfilled the quixotic wish of Ibn Saud, who wanted water more than oil for the kingdom he had founded out of a disparate collection of unruly desert tribes.

HAVEN IN A WASTELAND

From the days of camel caravans to the modern era of motorized vehicles, the spiky green of date palms set amidst an ocean of sand has always indicated the presence of an oasis—a refuge for hard-pressed desert travellers. The oasis at Najran, located in the south-west corner of Saudi Arabia, has for centuries been just such a haven of rest, refreshment and trade.

Nestled between two mountain ridges, 24 kilometres north of the Saudi Arabian border with North Yemen, Najran was for a long time an important stop on the ancient frankincense-and-myrrh trading route. Today it continues to be a centre of trade, serving the Bedouin who travel in from the desert specially to buy their provisions. It even produces enough food to sell elsewhere. Farmers irrigate their fields with runoff from the mountains or with water brought up from the aquifers—natural reservoirs found more than 90 metres below the surface of the ground.

Darkened by a shallow flow of runoff from the 3,500-metre-high Asir range, the Wadi Najran winds through the outskirts of the oasis. A dam in the hills above town controls the water flow to prevent flash flooding during storms.

Buildings clustered against an outcrop of boulders are enveloped by date palms; the trees, the original basis of desert agriculture, can survive and bear fruit on brackish water.

In a blur of pink, a little girl shoos a herd of goats through a date palm grove. The valuable trees not only yield nourishing fruit, but in some oases provide cool shade for crops.

At one of Najran's wells a man in white scoops up a mouthful of fresh water, pumped in a gushing torrent into an irrigation channel.

In fields outside Najran, workers harvest a bountiful crop of tomatoes; alfalfa, wheat, barley, aubergine and watermelon are also grown–primarily for local consumption.

A pair of wide-eyed children peer from a brightly painted doorway in a mud house in the old section of Najran. The population of the oasis–Najran proper, plus a series of smaller villages–totals nearly 50,000.

A prosperous Najran car salesman enjoys a whiff of incense in his comfortable reception room; behind him is a wall-hanging embroidered with verses from the Koran.

A mud-brick skyscraper shows Yemeni influence in its window decoration—yet sports a modern air conditioner.

While a goat noses into a wheelbarrow in the courtyard below, cloth dries on the flat roof of a house in old Najran.

A rooftop breakfast for two brothers
dressed in spotless white consists of
milk, cheese and loaves of bread.
Najranis enjoy eating on their roofs,
and also use the sunny areas for drying
vegetables and cleaning rugs.

A woman prepares loaves of flat bread
to be cooked on a rooftop griddle; in the
background, beside a pile of firewood,
is an oven for roasting nuts.

111

At a shop overflowing with imported fabric *(top)*, a man examines a bolt of blue cloth. Elsewhere in the *suq*, or market, in old Najran, a man wearing a red headdress *(above)* steadies a goatskin bag while the shopkeeper, holding a funnel, prepares to fill it with liquid butter.

In a general store stocked with soft drinks, canned goods and other sundries, a young assistant reaches into a milk cooler. The store is one of many in Najran, but not all have electricity to run refrigeration units.

As afternoon shadows lengthen, young soccer players get up a match on the outskirts of town, using the dry, sandy bed of the Wadi Najran for their field.

THE RISE OF THE SAUDIS

"It's hard for you to appreciate what development means to me," a Saudi construction-company manager told a Western reporter recently. "When I was 12, I studied by kerosene lamp. I drank water from a clay jug with little things moving in it. There were no doctors nearby. Today my son thinks deprivation is a house in Jidda without a video recorder."

To any Saudi of the generations preceding that of the construction manager's son, the tangible signs of material development are everywhere evident in Saudi Arabia. Barely half a century ago, there was no such thing as a national currency. Most people lived by herding and farming, just as their ancestors had for 2,000 years. Business transactions were conducted on a one-to-one basis by men who knew not only each other's faces but also each other's family pedigrees. Manufacturing was non-existent; most families made by hand whatever material comforts they had, from the tents over their heads to the sandals on their feet. Many a tribal elder and many a city merchant kept slaves as concubines, camel drivers, cooks, gardeners and wet nurses.

In the past half century, Saudi Arabia has undergone one of the most remarkable transformations of all time. By the beginning of the 1980s, government revenues and expenditures were in excess of $90 billion a year. Jet aircraft were screaming in and out of the nation's 20-odd airports every few minutes, carrying businessmen and diplomats from all over the world. Old cities were given new faces: in the ancient Red

Sea port of Jidda, bulldozers were clearing away row upon row of stately 200-year-old Ottoman houses of coral limestone to make room for modern high-rise buildings of steel and concrete.

New cities were materializing as if brought forth by a rub of Aladdin's lamp. The sites of two fishing villages at Yanbu, about 350 kilometres to the north of Jidda, and at Jubail, across the peninsula on the Gulf coast, are being transformed into metropolises. Designed to accommodate populations of hundreds of thousands each, they will possess everything from oil refineries, petrochemical plants and steel-rolling mills to yachting facilities. Despite lower revenues in the mid-1980s–owing to an oil glut on the world markets and falling prices–projects continue apace.

Saudi Arabia's industrial beehive is all the more remarkable for its occurrence in a society in which centuries-old unwritten tribal customs and the strictest of religious codes persist. The state operates without a constitution, without a parliament, without political parties. The head of state is the King–who is a version of the tribal elder of yore. He rules the nation by decree and holds power that is close to absolute–but only so long as he has the consent of the governed. If he reneges on his duties, he loses support and risks his position.

The constituency he must please consists of some 4,000 princes directly related to the late King Ibn Saud, the heads of other important tribes, and the *ulama*–religious leaders who are intimately versed in the Koran.

Saudi Arabia, more than any of the other countries of the peninsula, hews to a very conservative interpretation of orthodox Islam. The law of the land is the *sharia*, a collection of ninth-century writings that reflects the harsh viewpoint of the immediate successors to the Prophet Muhammad. Although it is sometimes honoured only in the breach, the *sharia* calls for murderers to be beheaded by the sword, thieves to have their right hands cut off, adulterers to be stoned to death and drunkards to be flogged.

To recount the emergence of this remarkable state requires separating a good deal of beguiling legend from facts that are in themselves almost incredible. By any reckoning, however, the story begins with Abd al-Aziz ibn Abd al-Rahman Al Saud, who created the state of Saudi Arabia out of a congeries of quarrelsome, feuding tribes for whom the concept of the nation-state had no meaning at all.

Abd al-Aziz, who was born about 1880 (the precise date is not known), began with a youthful vision. Family members later recalled that as a boy he would sit on a sand dune in Kuwait and gaze across the heat haze into the desert. His family had been exiled from Riyadh, 800 kilometres away, in the heart of the Najd–central Arabia. Even as a child, he was dreaming of reclaiming the home and the bygone glory of the Al Saud tribe.

Abd al-Aziz's forebears were Bedouin who in the 15th century had settled in the oasis of Dar'iyyah, about 15 kilometres north of Riyadh, which itself must have originated as an oasis, for its

5

name in Arabic means "date garden". There they stayed for 300 years, until lured on to a wider stage by the promptings of an 18th-century religious revivalist, Muhammad ibn Abd al-Wahhab, who saw it as his mission to create a society devoted to the strictest of Muslim teachings. Towards that end, he berated the Muslims of his day for worshipping demons and spirits, for wearing gold jewellery, and in general for straying from rigid observance of Islam as it had been preached by the Prophet Muhammad.

His preachings made him an outcast from his home village of Uyayna, north-east of Riyadh, but he found a welcome in Dar'iyyah, which was then ruled by an emir known as Muhammad ibn Saud–a direct ancestor of Abd al-Aziz. In 1744 the two men formed a pact, pledging to uphold and propagate the Wahhabi teachings together.

In the name of Islam and in alliance with the Wahhabis, the Al Saud warriors moved outwards from Dar'iyyah

and conquered surrounding territories–first the Najd, and later the province of the Hijaz on the Red Sea coast. By 1805 the elders of the two families held sway in most of the territories that today lie within the borders of Saudi Arabia. The Al Saud emirs gave military protection to the settled farmers, guaranteed the trading caravans safe passage, granted the Bedouin the use of wells and pasturing rights, and took tribute from all those groups. The Wahhabis served as members of the *ulama*

and as *qadi*, the judges who ruled on all religious matters.

During the course of the 19th century, the territories over which the Al Saud family and the Wahhabis held sway waxed and waned, for raiding was still a way of life in the Arabian Peninsula, and tribal alliances shifted like the desert sands. By the time of Abd al-Aziz's birth the Al Saud domains had shrunk to include not much more than the town of Riyadh.

In 1891, when Abd al-Aziz was about 11 years old, even that holding was lost. It was taken over by a rival tribe, the Al Rashid, who were pressing outwards from their tribal seat in Hail, located on the edge of the Nafud desert to the north-west. The boy's father, Abd al-Rahman, whose tribal alliances were no longer a match for those of the Rashid, fled with his wives, his brothers and their wives, and their respective children into the Rub'al-Khali.

For a time Abd al-Rahman and his family lived as nomads with the friend-

ly Al Murrah tribe. Then they settled 800 kilometres to the east with the emir of Kuwait. The emir found it expedient to encourage Saudi hopes for reclaiming their lost territory because he was himself a rival of the Rashid. Clearly the Kuwaiti elder's encouragement had an effect on the impressionable mind of the young Abd al-Aziz.

His chance to do more than dream on a sand dune came in September 1901, when Ibn Rashid, leader of the hated tribe, left Riyadh with most of his troops on a goodwill tour to Baghdad. Abd al-Aziz persuaded his father and the emir of Kuwait to let him make a dash for Riyadh with a small band of brothers and cousins.

By mid-October he had successfully raided a number of Rashid outposts, come within 150 kilometres of Riyadh and collected a band of fighting men from a number of tribes. But with December would come the Islamic month of Ramadan, a time when religious tradition decreed a cessation of raiding. Some of Abd al-Aziz's men lost interest in the venture and drifted away to their own tribes, but about 60 stalwarts remained at his side and followed him into temporary seclusion in the Rub'al-Khali. Here they camped in the parched sands, living on dates and camel's milk while they waited through the first weeks of Ramadan.

When the sacred month of Ramadan drew to an end, the band stealthily moved north towards Riyadh. On the first night of the new month, when the moon was conveniently no more than a sliver and all the Muslim world was preoccupied with celebrating the feast that ends Ramadan, they galloped their camels through the darkness. They swept over the rocks and scrubby growth on the plateau east of Riyadh and then down to the edge of the city, where they found the battlements undefended. Taking advantage of this lapse, Abd al-Aziz and his men scaled the walls and slipped quietly into town.

In the main square they saw the Mismak fortress, a squat and mud-walled construction that housed the Rashid garrison. Facing it was the mansion of the governor, an appointee of Ibn Rashid. A few doors down was a house that belonged to an old friend of the Saud family. Here Abd al-Aziz

Carrying banners proclaiming, "There is no god but God and Muhammad is his prophet," the Saudi Army moves across eastern Arabia in 1911.

ENIGMATIC HERO OF A DESERT WAR

Lawrence grasps an Arab dagger.

During World War I, Arabia's Turkish rulers were the allies of Germany. When the Arabians revolted against the Turks, the British gladly sent an officer, Thomas Edward Lawrence, to help them.

Lawrence of Arabia, as he came to be known, proved a brilliant leader of camel-mounted guerrillas. His daring raids behind enemy lines tied down large Turkish armies, inspired his followers to call him "Emir Dynamite" (for his liberal use of explosive), and made him a popular hero of epic proportions.

Lawrence was wounded 32 times, and once viciously tortured by the Turks. After the war he hid from the public, serving in the R.A.F. under an assumed name. In 1935 he withdrew to a country cottage, telling a friend that "there is something broken in the works... my will, I think." Soon afterwards he died, from injuries sustained in a motorcycle crash.

knocked on the door and—in addition to finding a warm welcome from his family's friend—learnt that the governor slept each night in the fortress and then crossed the square in the morning to breakfast with his wife.

With that information, Abd al-Aziz led his men up on to the roof of the friend's house, across the intervening rooftops and then down into the governor's mansion. There they seized and gagged the governor's wife and sister-in-law. Then they anxiously waited out the remainder of the night, passing the time by drinking coffee and reciting passages from the Koran.

Their patience was rewarded shortly after dawn when a small gate swung open in the Mismak fortress. The governor stepped through, and his bodyguards followed behind. Abd al-Aziz ran into the square, shouting, "God is great!" and firing his pistol. His cousin Abdallah bin Jaluwi sprang to his side and hurled a spear in the direction of the governor. It missed its target and lodged instead in the wooden gate of the fortress, where its steel point can still be seen today.

The governor tried to scramble through the gate but was thwarted by Abdallah bin Jaluwi, who seized him by the ankles and hauled him back into the square. At this point, the accounts conflict: Abdallah either knifed the governor, or shot him, or cut his heart out with a sword. But all accounts agree that moments later the governor was dead and that the Al Rashid garrison laid down its arms and surrendered to the young warrior.

Abd al-Aziz sent word to his father, who soon arrived from Kuwait and was welcomed with feasting and celebration. Instead of reclaiming the emirate for himself, as seniority entitled him to

do, Abd al-Rahman acknowledged his son's achievement by bestowing on him the ancient engraved sword that symbolized the tribal leadership. Abd al-Aziz, who had barely entered his twenties, was emir of Riyadh and of the Al Saud tribe.

The realm over which the young emir now ruled was primitive indeed. So meagre were his funds that he was able to carry his entire treasury in a single pair of saddlebags. But what he lacked in resources he made up in political skill and strong personality, which kindled the loyalties of Bedouin and villagers alike.

Touring the desert settlements and encampments, he proved to be a scintillating guest at tribal coffee fires, and he continued to win followers with his promise of adventure ahead and his dramatic retellings of triumphs to date. "A thousand camels on the march—a brisk, even pace—the murmur and buzz of the motion—the squeak of the saddles—a concrete body, moving, moving like a stream of water down a slope, without a single pause," is how one listener remembered Abd al-Aziz describing his movements in 1903. Within 18 months of the victory at Riyadh, Abd al-Aziz held control of towns and settlements 150 kilometres to the north and south of the city.

Success followed success, and by 1921 Abd al-Aziz was ready to take on Hail and the Rashids themselves. When he reached the town, the gates swung open and not a shot was fired as Abd al-Aziz marched in with his soldiers. The Rashids, as it happened, were quarrelling among themselves and had no will to resist the charismatic leader who in 20 years had won followers from all over the peninsula. Now they were to see for themselves

how he exercised his charm. First, in the desert-host style, he magnanimously ordered his rice sacks to be opened to feed the citizens. Next he summoned the incumbent Rashid emir to appear before him. Abd al-Aziz rose and embraced his adversary. "Sit here beside me," he said. "The time for death and for killing is finished. We are all brothers now."

Giving substance to that sentiment, he promptly bound the tribes together through matrimony. He took one Rashid princess for his own wife, gave a second in marriage to his brother Saud ibn Abd al Rahman, and a third to his eldest son, Saud ibn Abd al-Aziz. Thus in a single stroke he had ended the feud of decades—and at the same time doubled his own territory. To mark the

triumph, he assumed a new title: Sultan of Najd, indicating that he now ruled over central Arabia, more than half of the entire peninsula.

Within another five years he had extended his rule westwards as far as the Red Sea coast, where he took the all-important province of Hijaz, including the cities of Jidda, Medina and Mecca. As the most sacred city of Islam in the eyes of Muslims all over the world, Mecca was an especially valuable prize. It gave Abd al-Aziz great standing among Muslims everywhere.

By the end of the 1920s the bulk of the peninsula was under his command. The only exceptions were the sheikhdoms along the Arabian Gulf, where the British held protectorates for securing their sea route to India, and those of

the south-west, where the mountains of Yemen formed a natural boundary that had set the people apart since prehistoric times.

In 1932 Abd al-Aziz–or Ibn Saud, the name Westerners generally used in referring to him–formalized his conquest by bestowing the family name on the land he had secured and styling himself King of Saudi Arabia. He was ruler of the largest independent Muslim state in the world. The only foreigners to whom he would ever be beholden were the engineers and businessmen with whom in 1933 he signed concessions allowing them to prospect for oil in Saudi Arabia. The deals the King made with oil prospectors were solely business concessions, however, and they left him completely free to conduct

Located on the Red Sea 74 kilometres from Mecca, modern Jidda rises up behind its dhow-filled harbour. Since the 1940s, its population has swelled

from 30,000 to almost 1.4 million, more than half of whom are non-Saudis.

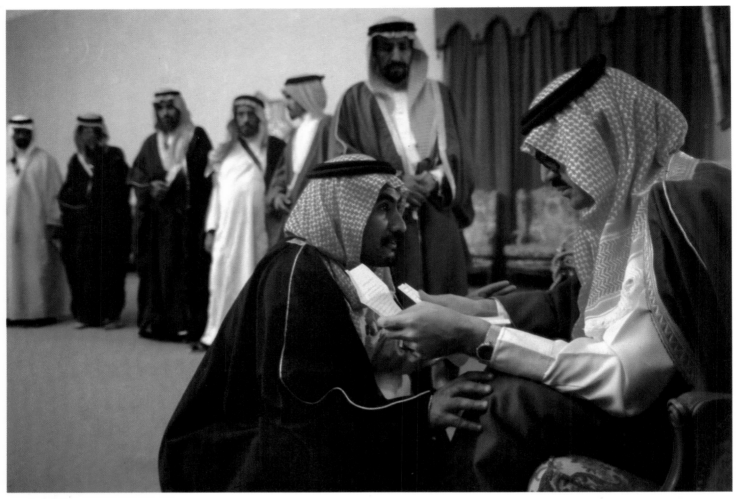

his government in his own way.

His own way was that of the traditional desert sheikh. For the next 21 years he consolidated his gains through the persuasive force of his own personality, the imaginative exercise of reason, the contracting of shrewd political marriages and the dispensing of desert largess—which now took on epic proportions. Some 500 visitors were entertained daily at lunch at the palace in Riyadh, and on a feast day to celebrate the end of Ramadan, the King gave away 3,000 gold-trimmed robes imported from Syria.

Ibn Saud's talents for persuasion were so compelling that they generated a number of apocryphal stories. One famous yarn told of how he persuaded religious leaders to accept the radio and the telephone. A pragmatic man, he was quick to perceive the value of communications devices for anyone with ambitions to rule over widely scattered peoples. In the early 1930s he had both radio transmitters and telephones installed in Riyadh and in Mecca. The religious leaders protested; to them it seemed that disembodied speaking voices must be carried through the sky by Satan himself.

According to the story, the King won the approval of the leading religious authority by means of an object lesson that was ingenious in its simplicity. "How far would Satan carry the word of God?" the King asked.

"Verily, you joke with me, for you and I know that Satan would never carry the word of God one inch," the religious leader replied.

"Then listen," said Ibn Saud. Doubtfully, the religious leader put his ear to the radio set (or the telephone, depending on the storyteller). Soon, through the growl of static came a voice reciting verses from the Koran. The religious leader gave a gasp of astonishment—and then promptly conceded that it must be God's own miracle.

Somewhat more complex, but vital

to his gaining the support of his people, was the use the King made of the institution of marriage. Islam allows a man to keep four wives at a time and permits divorce. No count has ever been made of Ibn Saud's wives and concubines, nor is it widely known how he dealt with those he tired of (in Saudi Arabia, a divorced woman usually goes back to her own tribe to be looked after by her father, her uncles or her brothers). At any rate, Ibn Saud had already made effective use of marriage as a political tactic at Hail, where he took three Rashid princesses as brides into the Al Saud family. Thereafter, he continued to wed the daughters of important sheikhs, so that by the end of his life every major tribe in the peninsula had forged a family bond with him. In a land where family ties are honoured above all else, the King could not have chosen a better way of securing the loyalty of his subjects.

The marriages served the further purpose of yielding him at least 45 sons. Those sons and their offspring have run the country since his death and have managed to hold it together in spite of the challenges that increased wealth and industrialization have brought. Among the most significant of the marriages he contracted in his early years was the one with Tarfah, the daughter of Sheikh Abdallah ibn Abd al-Latif, the *qadi* of the Wahhabi family in Riyadh. By that marriage Ibn Saud produced the future King Faisal–the most religious of his sons, and the one who more than any of the others was to help maintain a balance between the family's various factions and to promote pan-Islamic peace throughout the entire Middle East.

When King Ibn Saud died in 1952 in his seventies, he was buried in accordance with Wahhabi practice, in an unmarked grave in the desert. The monarchy passed first to his eldest son and designated heir, 51-year-old Saud ibn Abd al-Aziz Al Saud.

The nation Saud inherited was falling into debt–though just how badly would be hard to determine, for his father had kept only the sketchiest of accounts. "The old King didn't know the difference between a thousand and a million," said a Lebanese contractor. He had treated the country's oil income as his own personal spending money, using it to provide the gifts he flung about so prodigally.

The new King–big, placid, amiable Saud–turned out to be even more of a spendthrift. Like his father before him, he gave away immense sums to secure the loyalty of his people. But unlike his father, he had an insatiable appetite for opulence. He also undertook some ill-conceived attempts to modernize the Saudi kingdom.

Indulging his own whims, he toured the country with a caravan of no fewer than 50 vehicles, and held his public audience, or *majlis*, in an enormous custom-built trailer that had gilded armchairs, gold bathroom fixtures and a king-sized velvet bed set beneath wall-to-wall ceiling mirrors. As he rode through the streets of Riyadh he would toss handfuls of gold and silver coins out of the window and laugh with delight as he watched children gather them up from the dust. He erected a number of palaces, each more costly than the last and all of them spectacularly fitted out with modern novelties (the grounds of one included neon quotations from the Koran).

Saud's wish to modernize led him to found the first ministries for education, agriculture and water, and health. But these steps towards modernization only compounded his difficulties. Instead of appointing his brothers and cousins as the heads–a logical extension of tribal practice–he all too often chose hangers-on who were out to make money, thus laying himself open to charges of corruption (he turned over the privy purse to his erstwhile chauffeur). Then he provided each ministry with a new building. Altogether, the buildings cost $200 million to construct, and $192 million of the amount had to be borrowed from the Chase Manhattan and other banks in New York, since not even oil was returning revenues large enough to finance such extravagant undertakings in the 1950s.

Five years after Saud's accession to the throne, Saudi Arabia was virtually bankrupt. International banks were refusing to grant credit; Aramco was forced to underwrite further loans against future oil income.

Saud's brothers and uncles feared for the future of the kingdom and all that they jointly stood to lose if it should founder. More than money was at stake. In 1952 the throne of Egypt had fallen to a military coup; in 1958 the monarchy of Iraq was overthrown and three members of the royal family were assassinated. Signs of unrest also began to show up in Saudi Arabia; anti-monarchist slogans appeared on the palace walls in Riyadh, and labour strikes beset the oil fields. Saud, who had neither appetite for administration nor political skill for pacifying differing factions, was unable to deal with the problems that faced him.

His brothers and uncles, their instincts for tribal consensus surfacing, tried various means over the next five years to persuade him to appoint them to the government ministries and dele-

125

A driver with car trouble on a lonely highway uses a solar-powered radiotelephone to contact the nearest garage. Such telephones are used by nomadic tribesmen as well as automobile travellers.

gate real authority to them. Time and again Saud would yield and then renege on his promises.

Members of the royal family maintain a discreet silence about the events of those years, but it is known that at length—with the support of the *ulama*, in whose good graces they were ever careful to remain—they reluctantly issued an ultimatum that had the effect of deposing Saud. Grudgingly, he handed over power to his younger brother Faisal in November of 1964 and boarded a plane bound for Athens. He spent the remaining four and a half years of his life in exile in various ports of the Mediterranean.

Faisal was a felicitous choice for King. Of all the senior princes, he had just the right balance of character and experience to restore a sense of well-being and to ease the kingdom into the modern world. In appearance and in manner he was the very opposite of the corpulent and self-indulgent Saud. Tall and lean to the point of emaciation, Faisal had down-twisting lips that on occasion would break into a sudden, wry smile—as though, said one observer, he had been sucking a lemon and discovered something sweet inside. His deep religious convictions were accompanied by a natural asceticism. As Crown Prince he had chosen to live in a modest villa with his family rather than in a palace; as King he frequently drove his car to work. There he laboured long hours at his desk, sifting through the paperwork and attending to the kinds of details that had bored and mystified his brother Saud.

Faisal lived by routines so unvarying that associates jested about him out of his hearing. Ahmad Saki Yamani, who as Minister of Petroleum shared many a meal with Faisal, noticed that day after day at the end of dinner, the King would pick up an apple from a bowl, examine it carefully, return it to the bowl and examine a second, and return that one as well. When he finally chose an apple, he would set it on his plate, peel it, core it and section it, then eat it section by section and finally dip his fingers in a finger bowl. When he timed the procedure by his watch, Yamani discovered that from fruit bowl to finger bowl precisely seven minutes elapsed—it was never more, never less.

Faisal came to the monarchy well prepared. His father had begun sending him on goodwill tours abroad in 1918, when he was only 14, and subsequently appointed him the country's first foreign minister.

Since then he had proved he could get things done. During the reign of his brother Saud, he had overseen the treasury; in that role Faisal found that ready cash for current expenses had dwindled to 317 riyals—less than $100. So he launched a rigorous austerity programme. He slashed government appropriations, cut the royal family allowances by two thirds and prohibited the importation of such luxuries as Cadillacs. In just nine months the government's cash reserves climbed to a healthy 60 million riyals ($126 million), the budget was balanced, and the foreign debt was in hand.

When he became King, Faisal put into effect a 10-point plan for reforming the Saudi government. There would be government regulation of commerce

Much like a camel seller of old—except for the electric megaphone—a used-car dealer extols his models. Despite its wealth, Saudi Arabia still ranks low in car ownership; in 1980 there was one automobile for every 45 people, compared with one for every two people in the U.S.

These Saudi students need no veils because girls' schools are off limits to men, except for some religious instructors–who are blind. Even the nation's director of female education, a man, cannot visit his schools while students are present.

and banking to guard against the possibility of bankruptcy. Slavery was abolished; the government compensated 4,000 slave owners $2,800 for each slave freed. (Some of these slaves chose to remain with their former owners, working, as they had done before, as chauffeurs or nannies.)

In a bid to neutralize the differences between conservatives, who were beginning to deplore the encroachment of Western ways, and young radicals, excited by cries of nationalism coming from Egyptians in Cairo and Iraqis in Baghdad, Faisal said: "Like it or not, we must join the modern world and find an honourable place in it." Indicating that he intended to determine the pace of the revolution himself, he declared: "Revolutions can come from thrones as well as from conspirators' cellars."

One of the principal hindrances to modern development was the lack of a national infrastructure–roads, ports, water and sewage systems, electricity grids, radio and television stations, schools and hospitals. Instead of approaching the problem impetuously, on an ad hoc basis, as Saud had done, King Faisal launched a carefully calculated programme of development.

In 1965 he initiated the country's first television broadcasts. In 1970 he inaugurated the first of a series of Five-Year Plans that were designed to promote the technological development of the country. Interest-free loans were made available for the asking, and Saudi Arabians by the thousands rushed to take part in the programme.

By the end of the first plan, in 1975, more than 9,500 kilometres of roads had been surfaced–compared with only 240 kilometres in 1955. Some 75,000 housing units had been built. There were 62 hospitals with a total of

7,734 beds. Health centres and rural clinics proliferated throughout the country. One effect of the resulting improvements in health care was that life expectancy rose an astonishing 50 per cent, from 30 to 45 years.

No phase of the modernization effort did King Faisal take more seriously than education. More than 1,300 primary and secondary schools were opened during his reign, and so were a number of vocational training centres. In addition, he made scholarships available for those who wished to go on to university level.

He even sought to promote the education of women, something that had to be done with the utmost delicacy to avoid ruffling the prejudices of the religious hierarchy and the conservative elders. The true pioneer in this endeavour was the favourite of his three wives, the forward-looking Iffat.

As early as the 1940s Faisal and Iffat had broken with tradition in the matter of education by sending their own sons to schools abroad and by employing

A youth's jacket identifies him as a student at the University of Petroleum and Minerals, Saudi Arabia's most prestigious school. In 1930 there were only 2,300 students at all levels in the country, but by 1980 there were more than 1.5 million.

English governesses at home for their daughters. Then, in 1956, Iffat opened a school for girls in Taif, a fashionable suburb of Mecca. She was able to gather only 15 pupils that first year, for even the leading families were reluctant to entrust the training of their daughters to anyone but their mothers and aunts. But with Faisal's support, Iffat persisted, and eventually she won a grudging admission from the *ulama* that capable women would be needed by the country in such fields as nursing, child care and home economics. By 1974, more than a quarter of a million Saudi females were attending state-run schools and colleges.

Along with domestic reforms, Faisal launched some innovations in foreign policy. Soon after becoming King in November 1964, he started a series of trips abroad to the rulers of other Islamic nations. By September 1966, he had visited nine countries. Everywhere he went, he appealed to Muslims to join together in a Pan-Islamic bloc that would be capable of exerting influence internationally.

He did not make much progress towards unity then. But the crisis produced by the war between Egypt and Israel in 1973 brought Saudi Arabia into international prominence and inspired the Islamic nations to stand together for the first time. Afterwards, whenever anyone suggested to him that oil wealth had had more to do than Allah with the coalescence of the Islamic nations, Faisal would fix his melancholy eyes on his interviewer and solemnly ask: "Who do you think gave us the oil in the first place?"

By 1975 Faisal had brought Saudi Arabia into the modern world. The budget was balanced, the monarchy had proved to be stable, Saudi Arabia

had won prestige in the Middle East and the West alike and–thanks to the unflinching stand he had taken with respect to the production and sale of oil in 1973–oil prices were climbing.

Then tragedy struck. Faisal was holding his early morning *majlis* on March 25, 1975 when, from out of the crowd stepped one of his nephews, 26-year-old Faisal ibn Musa'id, the son of the King's younger brother Musa'id ibn Abd al-Aziz. As the King leaned forward to welcome his nephew with an avuncular embrace and kiss, the young man pulled a small pistol from under his *thawb* and fired three shots. The King was immediately rushed to the hospital in Riyadh, but the doctors could do nothing to save his life; within an hour he was pronounced dead.

The assassination sent shock waves of dismay throughout his kingdom. The Saudi Arabian announcer who had to report King Faisal's death over the radio broke off in sobs, reflecting the grief of his countrymen. The assassination made no sense. On the whole the Saudi people approved the progress Faisal's administration had made, and his sudden removal made it seem as though the great promise for the future had been withdrawn.

Some Arabians feared that the shooting might have been part of an attempt to overthrow the government, but such notions quickly evaporated. The assassin had a history of having been bounced from college to college in the United States. He had been charged with drug offences in Colorado and been in a barroom brawl with a girl-friend. The King had reprimanded him for his misbehaviour and ordered him back home in disgrace.

After the assassination, his uncles questioned the young man rigorously for two weeks and eventually reached the conclusion that his act reflected nothing more than his own mental im-balance. In deciding his punishment, they honoured the letter of the law as scrupulously as they would have had he not been part of the royal family: they had him publicly beheaded.

The transfer of power was carried out in an orderly fashion. Faisal's 63-year-old brother Khalid, who had

5

served as Crown Prince, became King; and another of the brothers, 54-year-old Fahd, who had worked in Faisal's administration as Minister of Education and then as Minister of the Interior, was named Crown Prince.

Despite the lapse of two decades since his father's passing and despite two decades of oil and money, Khalid remained the classic desert Arabian. "I like the desert, the Bedouin, my hawks. I am not a politican," he said. His self-appraisal was less than accurate, for he was in fact a skilful politician of the best sort. The time he had spent among the Bedouin had made them his willing allies. And his personal piety (he carried a little green leather-bound copy of the Koran in a pocket of his *thawb* and was often seen reading it) earned him the

approval of the religious leaders.

If Faisal's reign established Saudi Arabia internationally, Khalid's was the one in which the kingdom for the first time began to use its oil revenues to diversify its economy. When Khalid took over control in 1975, a year and a few months had elapsed since Faisal's oil embargo; petroleum prices by then had quadrupled, and the kingdom's annual revenues were increasing exponentially. They would rise from the $25-billion mark in 1975 to $32 billion by 1978. Every hour of the day and night, the kingdom was taking in as much money as it had during an entire year in the 1930s. The government treasury was piling up more funds than it knew what to do with. So far it had taken the easy course of depositing the

cash in Western banks—and inflation wrought havoc with its value. Something had to be done to make that money productive for Saudi Arabia.

Khalid had in his younger brother Crown Prince Fahd the very man to spend it well. Fahd, who also functioned as First Deputy Prime Minister, channelled the bulk of the swelling oil revenues into a sweeping new Five-Year Plan. The major thrust of the programme was a multibillion-riyal effort to make use of the country's resources as a foundation for other industries–oil refining, natural-gas processing and petrochemicals. The second objective was to wean the Saudi economy away from exclusive dependence on oil by encouraging the construction and the development of plants such as steel-

rolling mills and aluminium smelters.

To get such enormous projects under way would have been challenge enough for a nation that was already industrialized. Compounding the problems for Saudi Arabia was a deep-seated aversion to the kinds of jobs on which industrialization would depend, many of them being menial in nature. No true Arabian feels comfortable in a position that is subordinate to anyone outside the ranking elder of his family or his tribe. "It is not easy to persuade our youths to become technicians," laments a Saudi official in the Department of Higher Education.

To build the new Arabia, the government was obliged to import most of its labour force from other countries. At the start of the 1980s there were approximately two million foreigners at work in Saudi Arabia, or more than a quarter of the total population. American and European engineers were in charge of designing the development projects, and an army of Yemenis, Palestinians, Egyptians, Turks, Indians, Pakistanis, Taiwanese, South Koreans and Indonesians were imported to do the construction.

The sudden rush of humanity, machinery and money that attended these vast undertakings ushered in a plethora of troubles. Port facilities at Jidda and at Dammam became so congested that cargo ships had to wait for as long as three months at anchor before they could get space at the docks to unload their cargoes. "We threw a little money on the problem and solved it," said Planning Minister Hisham Nizer. The ports were upgraded, at a total cost of 6 billion dollars.

Meanwhile, inflation jumped to 50 per cent and the cost of living reached astronomical levels: three-room houses

in Jidda were rented for $45,000 a year in 1976. To alleviate the shortage of housing, the government underwrote a $300-million apartment complex–32 fifteen-storey buildings with such luxurious details as wall-to-wall carpeting and central air conditioning. But month after month the buildings stood empty, and local wags dubbed them the "Towers of Silence". One reason the apartments went unrented, so it would appear, was that the builders had neglected to provide the separate lifts for men and women that Muslim sensibilities demanded.

Without a doubt, money was creating as many problems as it solved. The new rich were spending their income on all-night binges with bootlegged Scotch, obtainable on the black market at $200 a bottle, and private showings of banned foreign films, some of them pornographic. Although indigenous Saudis were among the transgressors, foreigners–including other Muslims from countries that do not share Saudi Arabia's Wahhabi conservatism— came in for increasing criticism for their lax behaviour.

As outrage among the conservatives grew, tension mounted. The breaking-point came on November 20, 1979, the day that marked the beginning of the Muslim year 1400.

The start of a new century is cause for celebration all over the Muslim world. That day, some 50,000 pilgrims were gathered inside the courtyard of the Great Mosque in Mecca for dawn prayers. Shots suddenly pierced the air, and a voice rang out over the public-address system. "Behold the *Mahdi*!" the voice cried. There, at the centre of a cluster of supporters, stood a bearded young man. The speaker was claiming that this man was the messianic figure

tradition had long held would emerge from the desert to scourge the wicked and reward the virtuous.

"Recognize the *Mahdi*, who will cleanse the kingdom of its corruptions," the speaker continued. Thousands of terrified pilgrims tried to push their way to the mosque's 39 gates, but some of the more than 200 armed rebels who had concealed themselves in the crowd barred the way and locked the gates. More shots were fired, and a number of the pilgrims were killed. Islam's Holy of Holies, which the rulers of Saudi Arabia had vowed to protect, was under siege.

Manoeuvring with all the political skill at his command, King Khalid appealed first to the *ulama* for a strong censure of the disturbance. Then, with the moral authority of that august body on his side, he ordered in the Army and the National Guard. To the horror of Muslims everywhere, weeks of fighting ensued as the military forces tried to dislodge the would-be *Mahdi* and his band of zealots. The rebels retreated to a warren of passageways beneath the courtyard, making it even more difficult to root them out. By the time the shooting was finished, 127 soldiers had been killed, along with 117 rebels.

The government thought at first that the seizure of the mosque was part of a larger plot, the opening salvo of a major rebellion, perhaps one inspired by the Ayatollah Khomeini, a fundamentalist Muslim whose inflammatory preachings had only recently helped depose the Shah of Iran. But when the Army finally dragged the exhausted and weeping Meccan zealots out and sent them in handcuffs to be interrogated before having them publicly beheaded, it became clear that they had acted alone. Their leader, a wild-eyed former

A man-made arm of sandy beach embraces a swimming area at Jubail, the Saudi city being built on the Arabian Gulf by the American Bechtel Corporation. Some 1,600 Bechtel employees are managing the work of 41,000 labourers from 39 countries.

5

divinity student named Juhayman ibn Sayf, was simply a Wahhabi who had taken it upon himself to declare a *jihad*, or "holy war", against the modern state. The source of his anger was the royal family's close involvement in big business and the corrupting ways of the foreign workers.

In the aftermath of the crisis, however, the power of the royal family remained secure–partly because Khalid had made a point of getting the *ulama* solidly behind him, and partly for more personal reasons. Just as his celebrated father might have done, he dispensed largess among the soldiers who had quelled the disturbance–watches, colour television sets, cassette players and even cars. Those who had been wounded received special attention: he visited the hospitals where they lay stricken, he listened to the doctors' descriptions of their treatment and he went from bed to bed looking at the wounded with tears in his eyes.

Khalid occupied the throne for almost three more years. During the course of his reign, he proved himself as able a leader as Faisal–faithful to his desert instincts, yet up to modern innovation. In addition to diversifying industry, he brought some 15 non-royal ministers into the government. He was troubled, however, by a weak heart, and it finally gave out in June 1982. Once again the transfer of power was orderly; Khalid was succeeded by Crown Prince Fahd.

Fahd picked up where his brother had left off. He continued to encourage the rush towards the new, taking pains to preserve the old values–or, as one Saudi prince put it, to achieve "modernization, not Westernization". At the outset, some observers viewed Fahd with reservations, for he shared with Saud a taste for luxury (as a prince, Fahd frequently repaired to a lavish villa he owned on the coast of Spain). But his heavy-lidded eyes conceal deep reserves of shrewdness and energy, and he works as hard as he plays. Even as Crown Prince he was known to spend hours at a sitting going through the papers on his desk; and as King, no matter how busy he is, he still finds time several mornings a week to maintain the tradition of the *majlis*.

Although Fahd's first year as monarch was generally low-key, he did make one dramatic move, far-reaching in its implications. In June 1983 at an international conference in Mecca, he called upon religious scholars throughout the Muslim world to examine the Koran-based body of laws encoded in the *sharia* and reinterpret them in the context of modern times.

The proposal was a bold one: not since the ninth century have the laws been reinterpreted. The result may be to weaken the hold of religious conservatives on Saudi life. Whatever the outcome is, it should help Saudis focus on the contradictions their oil wealth has brought them, and help them through the perplexities of modern living.

King Fahd and most of the princes around him intend to see that the inevitable changes are made with a minimum of trauma–cautiously enough to placate the Islamic fundamentalists, quickly enough to satisfy a new generation of Western-educated technocrats, and in a manner that will translate the Saudi oil bonanza into a lasting benefit for all citizens. "The human being plays the basic role in the development of his society," Fahd has said, "for wealth comes and goes, leaving the effort and sweat of man the only asset to develop a society."

TOGETHERNESS IN A FAMILY COMPOUND

Equality and a sense of kinship are held dear in Saudi Arabia, and living arrangements reflect this. Thus, when Saudi executive Fahd Ad-Dulaimi, his father and two brothers set out to build a family compound in Riyadh, they decided that it should have separate but matching houses for their families, as well as an elaborate central pavilion where they could meet in their leisure moments.

Each of the four men obtained an interest-free $100,000 building loan from the government (the total cost would be $1,764,700), and together they hired the architect and contractors. Because of Saudi Arabia's shortage of native-born workers, the actual construction had to be carried out by labourers from Thailand and Pakistan, tile layers from Sri Lanka, electricians from the Philippines, stonemasons from Yemen. A team of Frenchmen, working 16 hours a day, supplied the finishing touches–doing the fine carpentry, hanging wallpaper and sewing curtains and drapes.

The four houses are identical in every respect, even down to their furnishings. The communal structure consists of a kitchen in which the wives take turns cooking, a large dining room, a luxurious *majlis*, or salon, for entertaining guests, a room for coffee and a television room.

The compound is situated in an ideal location, close to the mosque, to the school attended by Fahd's four children and within walking distance of shops. In addition to a small garden (*page 134*), it has an enclosure for goats–kept, just as in days of old, for milk, meat and ritual sacrifice.

Saudi businessman Fahd
Ad-Dulaimi rests in the courtyard
of his new home.

Construction rubble partially blocks
the main entrance to the Ad-Dulaimi
family compound. Beyond the arched
communal section are four separate
houses for family members; each unit
has its own water tower.

Fahd Ad-Dulaimi gives the newly
planted eucalyptus trees and date
palms in his gardens a good soak, a
luxury in an arid land. They will
eventually provide cool shade.

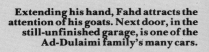

Extending his hand, Fahd attracts the
attention of his goats. Next door, in the
still-unfinished garage, is one of the
Ad-Dulaimi family's many cars.

The Ad-Dulaimi elder, a perfume
merchant, entertains in the comfort of
the just-completed salon. The baroque
furniture was custom-made in Italy.
The curtains and wallpaper are
French, the rugs Belgian.

Built as a showcase for Sharjah, one of
the seven pocket-sized sheikhdoms
making up the United Arab Emirates,
this shopping centre contains 600
shops but gets few customers. Sharjah
also has 10 under-used luxury hotels.

MIRACLES OF THE ARABIAN GULF

"I can order a drink at a bar, dance in a cabaret, read uncensored magazines or go to a film," a young man of Bahrain told a Westerner at the dawn of the 1980s. He was contrasting the free-and-easy lifestyle on the island of Bahrain with that of the strait-laced Arabs living on the mainland, hardly a half hour's sprint by boat or plane across the Arabian Gulf.

Citizens of Bahrain and the peninsula's four other Gulf states—Kuwait, Qatar, the United Arab Emirates and Oman—like to compare themselves with one another and with the Saudis. Part of that compulsion arises out of their race to join the modern world, as the miracle of oil transforms them from quiet backwaters to commercial centres of international importance. They are prone to a sort of tape-measure mentality that makes them monitor which among them has the tallest buildings, the largest airport, the deepest seaport, the most luxurious hotels, the biggest revenues, the best life.

Fundamentally, however, their rivalries are familial ones that long ante-date the oil age, for the people of the Gulf states share an ancient heritage. Indeed, the ruling sheikhs trace their lineages to the desert and have tribal ties with one another.

The major difference between the Gulf states and Saudi Arabia is that, by virtue of their location on the peninsula's east coast, the Gulf states had earlier exposure to foreign peoples than did the tribes of the interior. Members of the great trading families of the coast have throughout history made sea voyages to Iraq, Iran, Pakistan, India, Ethiopia and China. And agents of those regions have, in turn, made extended stays in Arabian coastal cities—as have a variety of Portuguese, Turkish and Dutch agents. Some of the visitors came not to trade, but with thoughts of conquering.

The last arrivals, the British, had no interest in what appeared to be the god-forsaken wastes of the interior and hence no motive for establishing colonial rule. But they were determined to secure the safety of the sea route to their all-important holdings in India. Beginning in 1820 and continuing into the 20th century, the British signed a number of treaties with the sheikhs who ruled the various tribes living along the Gulf. According to the terms of the treaties, the British pledged to come to the aid of any sheikh whose territory was threatened by a foreign power. As protectorates, the sheikhdoms—or emirates, as they were sometimes called—saw to their own internal affairs as before, with little or no meddling from the British. Nevertheless, the British were a presence for 150 years. The coastal inhabitants' exposure to foreign ideas explains in part their easier-going lifestyle.

Their differences from the populace of the interior do not run deep, however. The coastal peoples have more

6

in common with the Saudi Arabians and one another than their oft-invoked comparisons and sometimes quarrels might suggest. "We are brothers," says Qaboos bin Said, the Sultan of Oman. "Brothers quarrel, but their quarrels don't last long."

The Arabians have demonstrated this in the way they share the wealth that oil has brought them. The states that were quickest to reap the enormous benefits of the oil boom have been unfailingly generous to the others. Saudi Arabia pumped at least $600 million into Bahrain's national budget in 1982; in other years the United Arab Emir-

ates has given money to Oman, and Kuwait gives money to both Yemens. They do so in the spirit of the ancient tribal belief, reinforced by Islam, that no man is rich if his brother is poor. And in an extension of this tradition, they have been generous in helping other nations as well; Saudi Arabia, Kuwait, the United Arab Emirates and Qatar allocate part of their budgets to foreign aid for Third World countries.

Somewhat perversely, though good-humouredly, Bahrainis call themselves the "poor cousins of the Gulf"—perhaps because, at the height of the oil boom, they pumped a meagre 44,000

barrels of oil a day, while Saudi Arabia produced a prodigious nine million barrels and diminutive Kuwait one million. But in many other respects, the Bahrainis can consider themselves as leading the field. Bahrain was the first Gulf state to draw oil, the first to build an airport, the first to install a telecommunications system to connect itself via satellite with the outside world, the first to open a colour television station and the first to introduce public education.

Those firsts reflect a healthy and thriving society. For a population of 400,000 Bahrain has a hefty state budget approaching $1.5 billion a year,

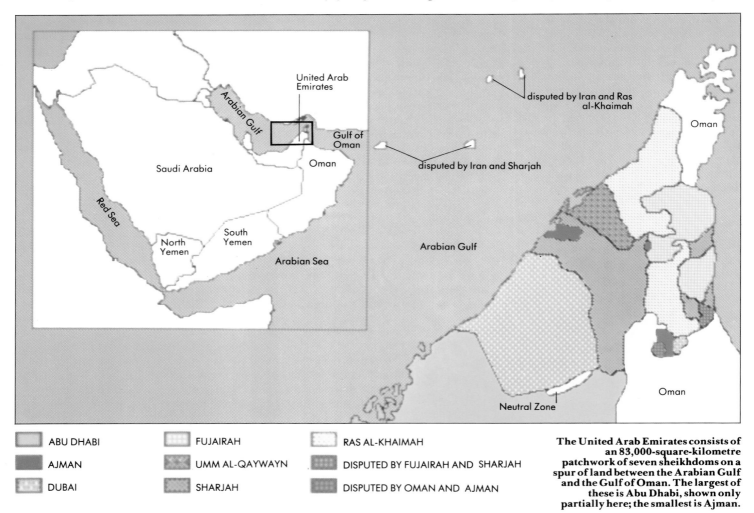

	ABU DHABI		FUJAIRAH		RAS AL-KHAIMAH
	AJMAN		UMM AL-QAYWAYN		DISPUTED BY FUJAIRAH AND SHARJAH
	DUBAI		SHARJAH		DISPUTED BY OMAN AND AJMAN

The United Arab Emirates consists of an 83,000-square-kilometre patchwork of seven sheikhdoms on a spur of land between the Arabian Gulf and the Gulf of Oman. The largest of these is Abu Dhabi, shown only partially here; the smallest is Ajman.

half of which goes towards developing projects that should sustain Bahrain's economy when the oil runs out, as it is expected to do in the 1990s.

One such project is a refinery that processes crude oil piped in from Saudi Arabia. Another is a dry dock that enables Bahrain to service supertankers that come from Norway, Germany, Korea, Greece and Iraq to collect oil not only from Bahrain but from the other Gulf states as well. Moreover, Bahrain has industries only indirectly related to oil—a rolling mill to process aluminium imported from Australia and a plant for processing iron ore from India, Brazil and Peru. Both industries use natural gas from the oil wells—and both provide Bahrain with a share in the construction industry that is thriving all over the peninsula.

Finally, not the least imaginative of Bahrain's undertakings is its involvement in international banking, which it began in 1975. "The area was ripe for a major banking centre of its own," says a British consultant to Bahrain's Monetary Agency, "a place where clients could deal freely in riyals and dinars as well as in dollars and sterling. Bahrain was a natural, located close to potential Arab clients and half way between the financial centres of Europe and the Far East. By working 7 a.m. to 7 p.m., we cover both money markets." By the early 1980s Bahrain had 20 local banks and some 70 international banks, and their combined portfolios totalled more than $23 billion.

Meanwhile, the standard of living for almost everyone is comfortable, and for many life is downright sybaritic. Many a deal between rich sheikhs and European, American and Japanese executives is struck in the bar of a luxury hotel—Bahrain has seven—or in the posh confines of the yacht club that overlooks the azure harbour of Manama, the capital city. And thousands of travellers from the mainland crowd the Thursday planes to Bahrain to enjoy a weekend of fresh and different air—bringing the island state another industry in the form of tourism.

About 300 kilometres north of Bahrain, on the borders of Iraq and Saudi Arabia, is Kuwait. It is the model that the others look upon with a mixture of envy and admiration. Kuwait has an area of scarcely 19,000 square kilometres—so small it can be driven across in two hours—yet is rated the world's third richest nation. Kuwait's known oil reserves are 70 billion barrels—estimated to be second in the world only to Saudi Arabia. By the start of the 1980s, oil revenues in Kuwait were running at $21 billion a year.

But Kuwait does not live by oil alone. It has been the most farsighted of all the Gulf states in parlaying its oil into even greater wealth. It has branched out from oil production and refining to manufacturing petroleum by-products such as liquid ammonia and chemical fertilizers. Additionally, it has started up light industries such as the manufacture of lead-acid batteries, salt, bricks, metal pipes and asbestos, and converted from its centuries-old dhows to steel tankers and container ships for handling the Gulf commerce.

Nor does Kuwait confine its investments to home. It has holdings in 500 U.S. companies and other investments in 45 countries around the world. Together, those investments earn Kuwait in excess of $10 billion a year.

Such enormous returns have redounded to the benefit of all Kuwaitis. There is no such thing as poverty in their country. As of 1983 the per capita income was $17,880, nearly half again as much as that of the United States and one out of every 230 Kuwaitis was a millionaire.

Amidst all that wealth, the government disburses its revenues to achieve what may be the most comprehensive welfare state on earth. "We want our people to be happy, and we can afford it," said the late Sheikh Abdallah al-Salim al Sabah. Practising what he preached, his government inaugurated a programme of subsidizing food and housing—which is equipped with free telephone service—and providing free medical care and free education right up to and including university level. Kuwait has its own university, but for promising Kuwaiti youths who prefer to study abroad, the government pays their fees and gives them each $2,000 a month to cover additional expenses.

In the field of public health, Kuwait spends more than $350 million to support 1,600 doctors, eight hospitals and numerous clinics. Its biggest hospital, Al Sabah, can handle everything from complex brain and open-heart surgery to kidney transplants.

Neither health nor wealth has given Kuwaitis the insouciance of their kin in Bahrain. Kuwait has 10 cinemas and two colour television channels (the latter show such American fare as *Dallas* and *Columbo*), but both films and television are censored so that no kissing, no bikinis and no unseemly language can offend Islamic mores. Kuwait has a race track, but no betting. It has nightclubs with bands, but no Western-style dancing and no alcoholic beverages.

Kuwaitis with a taste for flashier pastimes can easily go abroad to find them—and they do. One taxi driver, asked by a Western journalist how Kuwaitis bear the summer heat, replied:

An ammonia-and-urea fertilizer plant occupies a seaside location in the tiny peninsula state of Qatar. Despite its size, Qatar is industrializing to beat its dependence on oil production.

"I really wouldn't know. I'm usually in Paris myself."

In Qatar, 370 kilometres south on the coast, citizens like to travel, too, and by taking advantage of an unusual government bonus, they manage to see much of the outside world free. Qatar's welfare programme includes flying ailing citizens abroad for treatment. "Everyone who is sent to Europe to go to hospital is allowed to take a companion to look after them," one of the shrewder beneficiaries explains. "Usually it is a relative. But the regulations say only 'a companion'! So I have a friend who has to go for an operation at the London Clinic; I go as his companion.... I go with my friend from Doha to London and from London to Doha; altogether I visit 26... no, 27 countries. It just takes a little planning."

Qatar–a roughly 10,000-square-kilometre thumb jutting from Saudi Arabia into the Gulf–is so small that its entire native population of about 60,000 can fit into its sports stadium. Its oil reserves are only 1 per cent of the Middle East total, but even so they generate $2 billion in annual royalties. Those monies have brought the nation all manner of modernities: a new industrial centre that turns out, among other things, finished steel for export; a huge enclosed market that sells imported consumer goods, from Japanese radios to French bread and American soft drinks; and so much desalinated water that by the beginning of the 1980s daily water consumption in Qatar averaged 570 litres per person, about four times the European average.

Paradoxically, Qataris seem more determined than any other citizens of the Gulf states not to let go of their past. When women travel abroad, they abide so scrupulously by the Islamic proscription against baring their faces, that they refuse to be photographed even for passport identification, and they have the phrase "In purdah" stamped on their passports in place of photographs. Sheikh Khalifa bin Hamad Al Thani makes all ministerial appointments, mostly from among his kin, and all major decisions.

In tangible ways as well as in traditions, Qataris are preserving their heritage. The government has restored the palace of a 19th-century sheikh and turned it into a museum. On the front lawn stands a typical Bedouin tent, complete with clothes, cooking utensils, rugs and muskets. Inside are exhibits of waxwork figures depicting family life. Outside, in an ornamental pool, float fully restored antique dhows. Next to them, under guard, are three other artefacts not so indigenous but full of meaning for Qatari history: an old British Army truck and two 1940 Cadillacs–the first modern conveyances bought by the Sheikh at the dawn of the modern oil age.

Perhaps the state that most acutely reflects the anomalies and confusions attending the gusher of oil wealth is the United Arab Emirates, a confederation formed of seven tribal groups scattered along an 800-kilometre portion of the coast between the tiny peninsula of Qatar and Ras Musandam, at the foot of the Gulf. In 1971, when the British withdrew their military and political commitments, the emirates were too small to survive as independent states; some had populations of only a thou-

A ghetto for affluent foreign workers, this community of large houses with lawns forms a neat square in the desert just outside Dubai.

sand or two. But together they could muster a combined population of about 80,000. So they worked out a constitution that united them under one flag.

Two emirates–Abu Dhabi and Dubai–tend to dominate; the former has the lion's share of the oil and the latter has the best port. Their material advantages are reflected in the new political arrangement. The Sheikh of Abu Dhabi serves as President of the United Arab Emirates and the Sheikh of Dubai serves as Vice President. But the government consists also of a council, a cabinet and a national assembly in which the remaining five emirates are represented. And they all share in the oil revenues–about $15 billion.

In using their new wealth to bring their society up to date in a quarter of a century, the seven emirates now share the building and upkeep of common roads, telephone and postal systems, and defence forces. But age-old tribal rivalries have reasserted themselves.

The emirate of Dubai boasts that it has one of the busiest international airports handling more than 2.7 million passengers a year. Just 16 kilometres away, Abu Dhabi has invested $325 million to build another airport for three million passengers by the end of the 1980s. Sharjah and Ras al-Khaimah also have airports competing for international trade, while Furjah is still engaged in building its own airport.

6

Those projects and their failings are symptomatic of a wider problem. The U.A.E. has more airports, deepwater ports, hotels, supermarkets, apartment buildings and cement plants than it can generate business for. It has rushed headlong into spending its wealth without applying the forethought of its more experienced neighbours Bahrain and Kuwait, which began reaping the benefits of oil as early as the 1950s.

Oddly enough, the state to come the most smoothly of all into the oil age is one that got off to a late and uncertain start–Oman, on the south-eastern edge of the peninsula, with a detached portion jutting into the strait of Hormuz.

Oman's oil did not start flowing until 1967, and even then very few of the royalties were spent until 1970. The reason was that the state's ruler, Sultan Said bin Taimur, was a despot of unstable emotions and contrary ideas.

Said had a paranoid distrust of paper money in particular, and of Western influence in general. He hoarded gold coins in the cellar of his palace. He forbade his subjects to possess radios, cars, bicycles, air conditioners and sunglasses. He once sent a messenger to chide the British consul for smoking on the consulate balcony. He did suspend his xenophobia just enough to send his son and heir apparent, Qaboos bin Said, to Sandhurst Academy for a British military education–but when the youth returned to Oman, the Sultan kept him under house arrest for three years, believing he had been "corrupted" by British life. To underscore the point, he destroyed a collection of Gilbert and Sullivan records his son had brought back.

But the young man proved more than a match for his father. In the late 1960s, dissident tribes in the Dhufar mountains launched what was to be a long and costly insurrection against the Sultan, supported by Chinese and Soviet aid channelled through neighbouring South Yemen. By 1970 the rebels had surrounded the city of Salalah, the capital of the province. Qaboos recruited Jordanian and Iranian troops, Saudi money, and British officers and planes. With their help he stemmed the rebellion, seized the throne and put his father on a plane for London, where–perverse to the end–the old man lived in Western splendour in Claridges Hotel until he died two years later.

The realm that Qaboos inherited was a model of medieval anachronism. In 1970 Oman had only 5 kilometres of paved roads in its 220,000-square-kilometre territory. The capital city of Muscat was a walled warren of mud brick. "The city gates were bolted each night from eight until dawn," a visitor was told a dozen years later. "If you walked the streets by night, by law you had to carry a lantern."

Qaboos pledged to bring his country into the 20th century, and he did. He transformed Muscat into a modern urban complex. He installed electric streetlights. He dredged the ports and made them fit to accommodate supertankers. He paved and graded 2,400 kilometres of roads–and imported 80,000 cars and trucks to drive over them. He built schools, hospitals and health centres, brought in colour television and air conditioning–and in his private quarters he replaced his collection of Gilbert and Sullivan records.

Qaboos has made all these innovations without sacrificing old traditions. He receives visitors in an office scented with locally grown frankincense, and on dress occasions he bedecks himself in a purple silk turban, white robe and

Thousands of concrete knuckles, used in breakwater construction, crowd dockside facilities at Mutrah in Oman. This man-made deepwater port is able to handle more than 1.3 million tonnes of cargo each year.

LIFESTYLE OF A MERCHANT PRINCE

One of the richest men in the Gulf states is Abd al-Wahab Galadari, a Dubai businessman whose family emigrated 60 years ago from southern Iran to what is today the Emirates. Long before oil became the dominant source of the region's wealth, the merchants of Dubai maintained an extensive trading relationship with Europe and India, and the Galadaris built a fortune on this trade.

The second of three brothers (whose trio of villas is shown on the right), Abd al-Wahab Galadari attended the American University of Beirut. Then, after gaining several years' banking experience in Dubai, he began building his own empire in the mid-1970s by setting up the Union Bank of the Middle East (UBME). In its first full year of operation, UBME ranked in the top 60 among Arab banks. Within a short period it opened three branches in Pakistan, primarily to handle remittances from the large numbers of Pakistani workers in Dubai.

While retaining a controlling interest in UBME, Galadari has diversified in a number of areas, from international construction to real estate, a daily English-language newspaper and a Citroën car agency. One of his most ambitious ventures has been a $130-million complex that includes a hotel, offices and flats, and a revolving restaurant and ice rink. The complex is part of his plan to "make Dubai the business key for the whole Gulf area".

Like most of Dubai's wealthy, travelled élite, the Galadaris have embraced many Western customs. Mrs. Galadari wears no veil, and in contrast to many women of the peninsula, she allows herself to be photographed *(inset)*.

On the outskirts of Dubai City, the Galadari brothers live in matching luxury villas, with pools,

Abd al-Wahab Galadari, flanked by his wife and sons, stands in the flagstone courtyard of their home *(below, left).*

well- watered strips of lawn and the Arabian Gulf at their back doors.

One of the Galadari family's most valuable and prized possessions, this model steamship, made of solid gold, stands in illuminated splendour outside the door of their palatial banquet room *(right)*. Mrs. Galadari bought the ship at an auction in India.

An arrangement of tulips and daffodils forms the centrepiece on the Galadaris' intricately inlaid banquet table. Like the golden ship model above, the table, the ornate dining chairs and most of the home's other elaborate furnishings originally came from the palaces of Indian maharajas.

Fine china graces a lace-covered table in the family dining room, where daily meals are eaten with gold cutlery.

6

gold-embroidered black cloak.

Even in looking to the past, however, Qaboos finds lessons for the future. Oman is endowed with natural resources other than oil–among them, the copper that underpinned the ancient Sumerian civilization, and a more recently discovered metal, chromium, a vital ingredient of high-tensile steel for jet aircraft. Sultan Qaboos has seen that his country makes the most of them. He has revived the prehistoric copper industry, gearing up the Oman mines to produce 18,000 tonnes a year

by the mid-1980s. He has also begun mining and stockpiling the chromium ore for future export.

Oman has had to be more cautious with its oil revenues than the other Gulf states, not only because it has less oil than some of the others, but also because it has a pressing need for defence. It budgets almost 40 per cent of its expenditures to keep a 20,000-man force trained by British military specialists and equipped with the latest weaponry. Oman's need for defence is acute because neighbouring South Yemen, with

its ties to China and the Soviet Union, poses a worrying threat. And Oman's crucial position at the Strait of Hormuz, which separates the Gulf from the Arabian Sea, gives it special responsibility. About two-thirds of the world's sea-borne crude oil passes through the strait day after day as tankers exit from the Gulf en route to Europe, the United States and Japan–making Oman the sentinel for its fellow states and the precious oil on which they all depend.

Quite apart from sharing a common concern over the security of the oil itself, the Gulf states share a number of other concerns arising out of the billions upon billions of dollars that oil has put at their disposal. One is how to spend their money to earn more money–and do it without risk to their economic soundness. The Kuwaitis, who were the first to plunge into the sea of high finance, nearly drowned, thereby providing a bitter object lesson for themselves and the rest of the Gulf.

In 1977 Kuwait opened a stock exchange, the first in the Gulf, and it proved to be a stunning success. In four years the price of shares traded on it rose by 56 per cent.

But in the get-rich-quick atmosphere of the era, there sprang up a second stock market, the Suq al-Manakh, named after a plot of land where camels used to be watered, and where cars are now parked. The market was unofficial and unregulated. It quickly attracted a wide clientele that included big merchants and the members of the ruling family who were already legitimately investing on the official exchange but who came here because the returns were so phenomenal. Between May 1981 and May 1982, one index of share prices rose from 275 to 920.

As news of the market's high gains spread, the Kuwaiti investors were joined by a swarm of speculators who came in from Lebanon and Saudi Arabia, reportedly carrying suitcases filled with money. They bought huge blocks of shares at high premiums, paying with postdated cheques and expecting to resell at high profits before presenting their cheques for payment.

For a while everyone made money. But eventually it became apparent that, as collateral for their postdated cheques, investors were putting up shares in oil and other vital companies,

and the government took alarm. Fearing that the speculation would undermine the soundness of the official stock market and ultimately would undermine the state itself, the Central Bank, Kuwait's federal reserve, ordered banks to cease granting loans for postdated cheques and not to accept stock in Gulf companies as collateral.

Inevitably, rumours of trouble erupted, and suddenly in the autumn of 1982 there was a run on the banks as speculators rushed to cash in the postdated cheques they had been holding. The government reacted by suspending trading on the Suq al-Manakh and launching an investigation.

The revelations were astounding. All told, more than $90 billion of the postdated cheques proved to be worthless. Equally astonishing, it was discovered that about two thirds of the total sum was owed by no more than eight speculators. One especially, Jassim al-Mutawa, who had formerly held a job as a $900-a-month government clerk but was a member of a well-known Kuwaiti family, owed a staggering $9 billion in postdated cheques.

The Kuwaitis made light of the hullabaloo, dubbing the biggest speculators the "eight cavaliers" and jesting that London's Madame Tussaud's had sent an envoy to get Jassim al-Mutawa's measurements so that they could put his likeness in their waxworks as a specimen of the biggest single bankruptcy in history. Jassim took the jests in good humour, saying with a smile, "They are welcome." But for the government the affair was no joke. It had to act to keep the regular stock market from collapsing under the weight of the debacle, but it faced a delicate problem–whom to bail out, whom to send to gaol. At length the government bailed

out approximately 6,000 investors with debts of $7 million or less by creating a fund of several billion for loans to help them repay their debts.

Taking a harder stand on the investors whose worthless cheques made them guilty of fraud, the government froze the assets and seized the passports of Jassim and 62 other big speculators. Each one was put on a government allowance of $5,200 a month and then charged with paying off his debts. Meanwhile, the incident "divided families and neighbours," said a Kuwait professor. "In old Kuwait, if someone went bankrupt, everybody tried to help him. Today it's brother against brother and cousin against cousin."

Among the most widespread of problems common to the Gulf states–and to their larger neighbour, Saudi Arabia–are those associated with foreign workers, who from the beginning have provided the underpinnings of the oil economy. When the oil boom first hit, the peninsula states lacked the labour force needed and the technical and managerial skills demanded by the huge modernization projects they aspired to. In 1940 almost 50 per cent of the population was illiterate. But even the illiterate–especially those who still maintained active ties with Bedouin life in the desert–looked upon physical work as beneath them.

The governments therefore met the demand by recruiting hundreds of thousands of foreigners. Following the precedent set by the oil concessionaires in the 1930s, the Arabians invite their workers to come under contract to do specific jobs for specified lengths of time–maybe a year or two, maybe 10. Whether the immigrants come as bank executives or construction labourers, computer technicians or hotel bellboys,

6

with advanced degrees or as illiterates, they are obligated to go home when the contract expires.

Far from declining with the technological advances of the oil boom, the numbers in the immigrant work forces have increased. By the early 1980s the Gulf states were so inundated by foreign workers that the Arabians had become minorities in their own countries. In Kuwait, 60 per cent of the 1.3 million inhabitants are expatriates of 117 different nationalities. In Qatar, foreigners outnumber citizens by 3 to 1. In the United Arab Emirates "you can spend an entire day," one European diplomat says, and "speak to 100 people without meeting one person who was born here, and to see one you have to look for him on the top floors of the sky-

scrapers or in the palaces along the seashore, or in London or Cannes."

Inevitably, such numbers have created problems, misunderstandings and worries for citizens and for the governments alike. Some Arabians fear the population imbalance is a "time bomb ready to explode" in social unrest. "An American engineer or an Arab earns as much as 2,000 Pakistanis put together," observes an Arabist. "Do you think it can last much longer?" Others worry that unchecked dependence on foreign labour will stunt the Arabians' development of their own skills. "The nationals do not participate effectively in productive activities," says one Arab official. Another observes: "A financially rich country with a weak human resource base is

poor, no matter how high its per capita gross national product."

Finally, many Arabians genuinely fear a loss of their cultural identity. "We live in a strange reality here," says Atif Wassfer, a sociologist at the University of the Emirates in Abu Dhabi. "Today my robe was laundered by a Pakistani, my breakfast prepared by a Korean. I had an interview with a Palestinian and I ate in a Swiss restaurant with an Egyptian professor. Later I will teach youngsters who grew up in English and French boarding schools, I will have dinner with an American manager, and I will finish the day with a whisky in the company of a Dutch scholar. It is difficult to live this way and hang on to one's own identity."

For one reason or another, Arabians

view the presence of all those foreigners with sentiments that range from mild discomfort to indignation. In 1982, a study conducted by two professors of Kuwait University, who polled 23,000 citizens of the Gulf states, indicated that 44 per cent felt that the presence of expatriates actually "threatened their economic well-being". A quarter of them believed that immigrants should be required to live in special compounds, be transported to and from their places of work, and be restricted to visit separate shops and separate restaurants–a way of life that, in the observation of an Italian journalist, amounts to "something between concentration camp and apartheid".

Restrictions on the immigrants have not reached those extremes, but for practical reasons of language and cultural taste, they do live in separate enclaves. They are generally paid in their own currencies. They save or send home most of the money they make–especially if they are unskilled labourers, who are required to come without their families.

Yet they are judged by Arabian standards–a fact that causes friction and misunderstanding on both sides. When a man from Pakistan and a woman from Sri Lanka were found in bed together, he was punished with a public whipping and three years in gaol; she was given two and a half years in gaol, and both were sentenced to be expelled after their gaol terms. In Arabian society premarital intimacy is one of the most heinous breaches of Koranic law and hence a crime against the state. Even the merest suggestion of intimacy brings down the wrath of the Arabian authorities. An Indian shop assistant was given 15 lashes for blowing a kiss from the palm of his hand to the boss's

wife. A Filipino man was given six months in gaol and then expelled from the Emirates for brushing past a woman on a bus–although the woman was clearly not an Arabian, since Arabian women are not allowed to travel on public transport.

In the emirate of Dubai in 1982, newspapers were featuring daily stories on such incidents, calling them "crimes of immorality" and casting them in such sensational terms that the United Arab Emirates Ministry of Information stepped in and urged the press to soft-pedal the issue of immigrants. From the standpoint of various governments, immigration problems are serious enough without having racist and nationalist passions inflamed.

Illegal entry is a particularly worrying matter. All immigrants are supposed to have visas and work permits, which can be obtained only when an employer guarantees a job and acts as sponsor. But many workers slip into the peninsula without observing the formalities. They are lured by the high pay; Sri Lankans, for instance, in Qatar can earn 27 times the wages they could earn at home, in Kuwait 37 times as much and in Bahrain 50 times as much. In the early 1980s, therefore, a number of the Gulf states discovered they had more workers present than were registered. The United Arab Emirates found that half its foreign population was in the state illegally; Qatar learnt that tens of thousands of workers had no sponsors, and Kuwait discovered about 100,000 foreigners in its midst under false pretences.

The Kuwaiti government promptly cracked down, giving all aliens two months to register and find sponsors or leave the country. The result was that government offices, embassies and em-

ployers were besieged, some with as many as 5,000 pushing and shoving applicants a day appealing for assistance. Some found sponsors and legitimate work, but eventually about 60,000 were required to leave. Some had to be evicted forcibly, and for a time the airport was the scene of deportees clutching bedrolls and Japanese radios as they waited for planes to take them away.

Whatever the headaches they cause the peninsula's governments and citizens, foreign workers are indispensable–and at all levels of the economy. As one Arabian official expressed it: "Were the Egyptians to be removed, many of the school systems would have to close; were the Palestinians to be forced to leave, the media would cease to function; were the British, Jordanian, Pakistani, Baluchi, Yemeni and Omani soldiers to be expelled, the defence and internal security network would collapse; were the Iranians, Baluchis and Pathans who make up the bulk of the labour force to be sent back to their homelands, progress on such vital development projects under way as the building of roads, ports, irrigation schemes, housing projects, schools and medical clinics would all come to an abrupt halt." Like it or not, Arabians are resigned to the presence of foreigners in their midst, and expect to be for some time to come.

The manpower shortage has inevitably brought to the fore an issue familiar to the West–women's role in society. On balance, the peninsula has been the scene of a dramatic evolution in the status of women. But the evolution has proceeded slowly and unevenly.

The hold that the old ways have on men and women alike is nowhere more apparent than in wedding celebrations. In 1981, Sheikh Zayid, ruler of the emirate of Abu Dhabi, threw a $40-million nuptial party to celebrate the marriage of his eldest son, Prince Muhammad. The bride's dowry included an entire town with three apartment buildings, a luxury hotel and 55 shops. The festivities included such extravagances as two million fireworks; Arab and African dance troupes; a caravan of 20 camels laden with trunks of diamonds, emeralds and rubies; and enough food to feed 20,000 guests for seven nights running. Throughout that gala celebration, the bride remained cloistered in her room in obedience to ancient tradition.

Her mother-in-law, Sheikha Fatima, takes an active part in adapting women's role to the new world of oil money. Fatima, who became Sheikha of Abu Dhabi in 1960, when she was a barefoot Bedouin girl of 13, has never been seen by any man other than her husband, father and brothers. She still masks her face with the *burqa*, even in the women's quarters of the palace. She has never been to a film or a restaurant and has never gone shopping. She spends the summer in London, but never leaves the house in which the family stays, except to take the·Sheikh's private plane back to Abu Dhabi.

But at home in the sheikhdom, Fatima is very active as president of the Abu Dhabi Women's Association and regularly leaves her palace to attend its meetings. The association, which was formed in 1973, has hundreds of members who teach illiterate desert women hygiene, handicrafts and the legal rights of women. It publishes a women's magazine and was instrumental in establishing one of the first branch banks for women.

The bank is managed, staffed and patronized entirely by women and has

almost 2,000 clients, the majority from Abu Dhabi and 60 per cent of them illiterate. The atmosphere has the hospitality of a desert tent. There are no counters. Clients drink tea or coffee and eat sticky cakes, and they transact their business in comfortable chairs set upon richly carpeted floors.

Sanctuaries such as this one evolved spontaneously, for despite the fact that women have always owned their own jewellery, household tents, camels and money–and retain those properties if they should divorce–banking per se has staunchly resisted any mixing of the sexes. Many hundreds of women now work in banks, but all in segregated quarters that deal only with women. Of the 300 members of the Arab Bankers' Association in the Middle East, only four are women. "There is a myth," observes one Arabian woman banker "that numbers, calculation and business aren't feminine."

The old pressures die hard, and not just in the conservative society of Abu Dhabi. Throughout the Arabian Peninsula, women defer to men in most aspects of their lives. Single women and divorced women without children are not expected to live alone, and going

out with men is forbidden. Noura Kassem, who in 1974 became the country's first woman inspector of schools, sighs: "My dearest wish is to see Qatari girls and boys sitting talking together."

Sooner or later she will get her wish, for little by little the signs of change are emerging. Although arranged marriages are still the custom, educated women at least now occasionally turn down their families' choices. Engaged couples, once forbidden even to see each other before marriage, sometimes get together in the presence of family chaperones. Women who earn university degrees are increasingly going to work in offices–and they go dressed in modest but fashionable Western clothes, not cloaked in the *abayas* that their mothers wear.

Insofar as the pace of female emancipation depends largely on the level and quality of a woman's education, the role of working women is likely to become more important. There are 17 universities, plus other institutions of higher learning, on the Arabian Peninsula, and none denies admission to women. Indeed, at the University of Bahrain, 90 per cent of the students are women, and Kuwait University has

Showing her modernity, an unveiled woman appears on a Kuwaiti television show. But such free expression goes just so far; when a woman commentator proposed on the air that women should be allowed to vote, she was censured.

more women than men–partly because so many Bahraini and Kuwaiti families still send their sons abroad to study. But Kuwait University leads the way in coeducational classes, and some are taught by women professors.

Not surprisingly, Bahraini and Kuwaiti women are the most emancipated of any in the Gulf states. They drive cars and travel freely, without escort, at home and even abroad. They appear on the stage and on television. They even work as salesgirls and secretaries, two occupations that are still frowned upon in many parts of the Arab world because they throw Muslim women into association with men not members of their own families.

Kuwait's women's movement is particularly strong and regularly sends a representative to the International Women's Conference. As early as 1970 Kuwait acquired its first woman doctor, a paediatrician who was employed at Al Sabah Hospital. Several women are diplomats in the Foreign Service, a woman is Undersecretary of Education, another is acting dean of the law school, and still another directs a television programme for women.

The Kuwait Oil Company even employs women engineers. One, with a degree in chemical engineering from the University of Colorado, heads the Operational Planning Division. Another, a graduate in mathematics, runs the advanced computer system. Asked to explain this novel record of distaff workers, a woman banker replied: "Kuwaiti women have strong personalities, and Kuwaiti men are therefore used to dealing with them."

The other states will have to get used to women, too. By the start of the 1980s, women had entered the work force all over the peninsula, even in the most conservative states. In Saudi Arabia, which resisted the entry of women

6

into the work force in the early days, Planning Minister Hisham Nizer reflected the changing view when he said: "The question now is what sort of jobs you are going to allow women to take, rather than whether or not they are going to work." In Oman, where the number of working women is small compared with the number working in the other Gulf states (a result of Oman's late entrance into the oil boom), Sultan Qaboos is encouraging women to be trained for the work force.

What is significant about the growing number of women in the work force is that few of them have to work to support themselves. In most of the states, if a woman has no male relative to provide for her, the government's welfare system does so. Women work out of a sense of wishing to do something to help their countries modernize and for personal fulfilment. The conviction that they should was well established as the 1980s got under way.

As the Gulf states modify their traditional attitudes towards women, so do they alter their views on other matters to adapt to the modern world. One of the most hopeful signs for the future is that the countries of the peninsula are trying to set aside their ancient suspicions and rivalries in favour of regional co-operation that could eventually bring about a kind of common market. The Gulf Co-operation Council, which was established in February 1981, introduced measures to reduce tariffs among the six nations and promote regional development. By pooling their resources, Common Market fashion, they would find it possible to undertake bigger projects together than they can do separately. The number of industries each state could then develop would increase.

The G.C.C. hopes also to prepare a common industrial policy to avoid the duplication of development projects that has occurred in the United Arab Emirates. To that end, it has proposed a computerized oil-data centre that will eventually service all six member countries. It will be located in Oman, which from its vantage point at the Strait of Hormuz oversees the exit of all tankers from the Gulf.

In addition, the G.C.C. is establishing a new university in Bahrain to complement rather than compete with the 17 existing universities in the region. According to Dr. Abdallah Rifai, Secretary General of Kuwait University and the leading figure behind the Gulf University project, the university will not be a carbon copy of existing institutions. "We will try to concentrate on programmes where there are shortages of personnel in society, such as medicine, and on subjects not much touched by other universities—for instance, arid-zone research, marine sciences, energy," he says.

What intrigues most observers, Western and Arabian, is the question of whether the headlong pace to develop industrially and economically will undermine Islamic ideals and customs. "Arabian women must go forward," says Sheikha Fatima of Abu Dhabi, "but at the same time not throw away all their habits and traditions." Add the phrase "and men," and most Arabians would share the same sentiment.

As they look to the future, Arabians throughout the peninsula are aware that much remains to be done. "The process of national regeneration," says Sheikh Khalifa of Qatar, "bears no resemblance to the lighting of a match, which is extinguished the moment after it is struck."

Rising from the desert, the domed buildings of Sharjah airport have proved a mirage of planning. The airport was built at a cost of one billion dollars to accommodate an expected burgeoning of international traffic, but handles under 50 planes a week.

ACKNOWLEDGEMENTS

The index for this book was prepared by Barbara L. Klein. For their help in the preparation of this volume, the editors wish to thank: A. Abushadi, The International Monetary Fund, Washington, D.C.; Abdul Aziz H. al-Swoayegh, Asst. Deputy Minister for Foreign Information, Ministry of Information, Riyadh, Saudi Arabia; George Atiyeh, Library of Congress, Washington, D.C.; Ruth Baacke, Malcolm Peck, The Middle East Institute, Washington, D.C.; Tom Barger, California; Glenn Brown, Reston, Va.; The Embassy of Bahrain, Washington, D.C.; The Embassy of Kuwait, Washington, D.C.; The Embassy of Oman, Washington, D.C.; Mr. Bogdady, The Embassy of Saudi Arabia, Washington, D.C.; Edmond Gharib, The Embassy of the United Arab Emirates, Washington, D.C.; Mark Hambly, U.S. Department of State; Jim Knight, Aramco, Washington, D.C.; Joseph Malone, Washington Research Inc., Washington, D.C.; Bill Mulligan, New Hampshire; The United States Geological Survey, Washington, D.C.; The World Bank, Washington, D.C.

The following sources were particularly valuable in the preparation of this volume: *The Nomads of the Nomads* by Donald Powell Cole, AHM Publishing Corporation, 1975; *Frankincense and Myrrh* by Nigel Groom, Longman Publishers, 1980; and *Arabian Sands* by Wilfred Thesiger, E. P. Dutton, 1959. Quotations from the Koran, translated by N. J. Dawood (Penguin Classics, fourth revised edition 1974; from pages 103, 209, 360-361, 366 and 368) are reprinted by permission of Penguin Books Ltd., copyright N. J. Dawood, 1974. Excerpts from *The Kingdom*, copyright 1981 by Robert Lacey, are reprinted by permission of Harcourt Brace Jovanovich, Inc.

PICTURE CREDITS

Credits from left to right are separated by semicolons, from top to bottom by dashes.

Cover: Pascal and Maria Maréchaux, Paris. Endpaper maps by: Lloyd K. Townsend, Maytown, Pennsylvania. Digitized by Creative Data, London.

1, 2: © Flag Research Center, Winchester, Massachusetts. 6, 7: Walter Schmitz from Bilderberg, Hamburg. 8-11: Pascal and Maria Maréchaux, Paris. Charts digitized by Creative Data, London. 12, 13: Anthony Howarth from Woodfin Camp, New York. Charts digitized by Creative Data, London. 14, 15: Robert Azzi from Woodfin Camp, New York. 16-19: Pascal and Maria Maréchaux, Paris. 20: Robin Constable from Quartet Books, London. 21, 22: Lynn Abercrombie, Shady Side, Maryland. 23, 25: Pascal and Maria Maréchaux, Paris. 26: Lynn Abercrombie. 28-38: Pascal and Maria Maréchaux, Paris. 40: Photo by Philip Pocock, from the Spencer Collection, The New York Public Library, Astor, Lenox and Tilden Foundations. 41: The British Library, London. 42: Photo by Philip Pocock, from the Spencer Collection, The New York Public Library, Astor, Lenox and Tilden Foundations. 44: Frank & Marie-T. Wood Print Collections, Alexandria, Virginia (2); photo by Philip Pocock, from the Spencer Collection, The New York Public Library, Astor, Lenox and Tilden Foundations. 45: Aramco Photo, Washington, D.C.; Lynn Abercrombie, Shady Side, Maryland; Raymond Depardon from Gamma-Liaison, New York– Robert Azzi from Woodfin Camp, New York. 46: Pascal and Maria Maréchaux, Paris. 47: Robert Azzi from Woodfin Camp, New York. 48: Lynn Abercrombie. 49: Hans Bollinger from STERN, Hamburg. 51: Pascal and Maria Maréchaux, Paris. 52-59: Robert Azzi from Woodfin Camp. 60-63: Pascal and Maria Maréchaux, Paris. 64, 65: Robert Azzi from Woodfin Camp. 66: Tor Eigeland, Barcelona. 67: Tor Eigeland from Black Star, New York. 68, 69: Tim Callahan assisted by Drew Hardy, from *Traditional Crafts of Saudi Arabia* by John M. Topham and others, published by Stacey International, 1982, John M. Topham. 71: Robert Azzi from Woodfin Camp. 72, 73: Pascal and Maria Maréchaux, Paris. 74: Robert Azzi from Woodfin Camp. 76-89: Pascal and Maria Maréchaux, Paris. 90, 91: Robert Azzi from Woodfin Camp. 93: Map by Bill Hezlep. Digitized by Creative Data, London. 94: The Imperial War Museum, London. 95, 96: Aramco Photo. 97-99: Robert Azzi from Woodfin Camp. 100: Lynn Abercrombie. 101: Robert Azzi from Woodfin Camp. 102: Tchekof Minosa-Scorpio, Paris. 104-115: Pascal and Maria Maréchaux, Paris. 116: Robert Azzi from Woodfin Camp. 118, 119: Royal Geographical Society, London. 120: The Imperial War Museum, London. 121-123: Robert Azzi from Woodfin Camp. 124: John Lewis Stage from Imae Bank. 126-130: Robert Azzi from Woodfin Camp. 133-135: Pascal and Maria Maréchaux, Paris. 136, 137: Robert Lebeck from STERN, Hamburg. 138: Map by Lloyd K. Townsend. Digitized by Creative Data, London 140, 141: Robert Azzi from Woodfin Camp; Robert Lebeck from STERN, Hamburg. 142, 143: Robert Azzi from Woodfin Camp. 144-150: Robert Lebeck from STERN, Hamburg. 152, 153: Robet Azzi from Woodfin Camp. 154, 155: Robert Lebeck from STERN, Hamburg.

BIBLIOGRAPHY

BOOKS

Alessa, Shamlan Y., *The Manpower Problem in Kuwait*. Kegan Paul International, London, 1981.

Almana, Mohammed, *Arabia Unified*. Hutchinson Benham, London, 1980.

Aramco Handbook, 1968. Aramco, Washington, D.C., 1968.

Arberry, Arthur J.:
The Koran Interpreted. Macmillan, New York, 1955.
The Seven Odes. George Allen and Unwin, London, 1957.

Bailey, Ronald H., and the Editors of Time-Life Books, *Glacier*. Time-Life Books, Alexandria, Va., 1982.

Bibby, Geoffrey, *Looking for Dilmun*. Alfred A. Knopf, New York, 1969.

Bulliet, Richard W., *The Camel and the Wheel*. Harvard University Press, Cambridge, Mass., 1975.

Chappell, Herbert, *Arabian Fantasy*. Namara Publications/Quartet Books, New York, 1976.

Congressional Quarterly, *The Middle East*. 5th ed. Congressional Quarterly, Washington, D.C., 1981.

Cottrell, Alvin J., ed., *The Persian Gulf States: A General Survey*. The Johns Hopkins University Press, Baltimore, 1980.

Detienne, Marcel, *The Garden of Adonis*. The Humanities Press, Atlantic Highlands, N.J., 1977.

Doe, Brian, *Southern Arabia*. McGraw-Hill, New York, 1971.

Dunlop, D,M., *Arab Civilization to A.D. 1500*. Praeger, New York, 1971.

Faris, Nabih Amin, ed., *The Arab Heritage*. Princeton University Press, Princeton, N.J., 1944.

Farsy, Fouad al-, *Saudi Arabia: A Case Study in Development*. Stacey International, London, 1978.

Flint, Richard Foster, and Brian J, Skinner, *Physical Geology*. John Wiley and Sons, New York, 1977.

Freeth, Zahra, *A New Look at Kuwait*. George Allen and Unwin, London, 1972.

Gray, Seymour, *Beyond the Veil*. Harper & Row, New York, 1983.

Groom, Nigel, *Frankincense and Myrrh*. Longman, New York, 1980.

Guellouz, Ezzedine, *Mecca: The Muslim Pilgrimage*. Paddington, London, 1979.

Hill, Ann and Daryl, *The Sultanate of Oman: A Heritage*. Longman, New York, 1979.

Hitti, Philip K., *History of the Arabs*. Macmillan, London, 1961.

Holden, David, and Richard Johns, *The House of Saud*. Holt, Rinehart and Winston, New York, 1981.

Holt, P.M., Ann Lambton and Bernard Lewis, eds., *The Cambridge History of Islam*. Vol 1. Cambridge University Press, Cambridge, 1970.

Hourani, George F., *Arab Seafaring in the Indian Ocean in Ancient and Medieval Times*. Princeton University Press, Princeton, N.J., 1951.

Howarth, David, *Dhows*. Quartet Books, New York, 1977.

Ibrahim, Saad Eddin, and Donald P. Cole, *Saudi Arabian Bedouin: An Assessment of Their Needs*. The American University in Cairo, Cairo, 1978.

Jeffery, Arthur, *Islam: Muhammad and His Religion*. Bobbs-Merrill, New York, 1958.

Katakura, Motko, *Bedouin Village*. Tokyo University Press, Tokyo, 1977.

Kay, Shirley, *The Bedouin*. David and Charles, Devon, 1978.

The Koran. Transl. by N. J. Dawood. Penguin Books, London, 1981.

Lacey, Robert, *The Kingdom*. Avon Books, New York, 1981.

Lancaster, William, *The Rwala Bedouin Today*. Cambridge University Press, Cambridge, 1981.

Lewis, Bernard, *The Arabs in History*. Harper & Row, New York, 1960.

Long, David Edwin:

The Hajj Today. The State University of New York Press, Albany, N.Y., 1979.

The Persian Gulf: An Introduction to Its Peoples, Politics and Economics. Westview Press, Boulder, Colo., 1978.

Long, David Edwin, and Bernard Reich, *The Government and Politics of the Middle East and North Africa*. Westview Press, Boulder, Colo., 1980.

Longrigg, Stephen Hemsley, *Oil in the Middle East*. Oxford University Press, London, 1968.

Malone, Joseph J., *The Arab Lands of Western Asia*. Prentice-Hall, Englewood Cliffs, N.J., 1973.

Mansfield, Peter:

The Arabs. Penguin Books, London, 1982.

The New Arabians. Doubleday, New York, 1981.

Maréchaux, Pascal, *Arabia Felix: Images of Yemen and Its People*. Barron's, Woodbury, N.Y., 1980.

Martin, Richard C., *Islam: A Cultural Perspective*. Prentice-Hall, Englewood Cliffs, N.J., 1982.

Monroe, Elizabeth, *Philby of Arabia*. Faber and Faber, Winchester, Mass., 1973.

Mosley, Leonard, *Power Play*. Random House, New York, 1973.

The National Geographic Society, *Nomads of the World*. National Geographic, Washington, D.C., 1971.

Nawwab, Ismail I., Peter C. Speers and Paul F. Hoye, eds., *Aramco and Its World*. Aramco, Dhahran, Saudi Arabia, 1980.

Nutting, Anthony, *The Arabs*. Clarkson N. Potter, New York, 1964.

Nyrop, Richard F., and others:

Area Handbook for the Persian Gulf States. U.S. Government Printing Office, 1977.

Area Handbook for Saudi Arabia. U.S. Government Printing Office, 1977.

Area Handbook for the Yemens. U.S. Government Printing Office, 1977.

Osborne, Christine, *The Gulf States and Oman*. Croom Helm, London, 1977.

Owen, Edgar Wesley, *Trek of the Oil Finders: A History of Exploration for Petroleum*. The American Association of Petroleum Geologists, Tulsa, Okla., 1975.

Polk, William R., and William J. Mares, *Passing Brave*. Alfred A. Knopf, New York, 1973.

Raban, Jonathan, *Arabia: A Journey through the Labyrinth*. Simon and Schuster, New York, 1979.

Raswan, Carl R., *Black Tents of Arabia*. Farrar, Straus and Giroux, New York, 1935.

Rauf, M. A., *A Brief History of Islam*. Oxford University Press, London, 1964.

Rodinson, Maxime, *Mohammed*. Pantheon Books, New York, 1971.

Salibi, Kamal, *A History of Arabia*. Caravan Books, Delmar, N.Y., 1980.

Sapsted, David, *Kuwait*. Macmillan, London, 1980.

Schmidt-Nelson, Knut, *Desert Animals*. Clarendon Press, Oxford, 1964.

Schopen, Armin, *Das Qat*. Arbeiten aus dem Seminar für Völkerkünde der Johann Wolfgang Goethe Universität, Frankfurt-am-Main. Franz Steiner Verlag, Wiesbaden, 1978.

Schurr, Sam H., and Paul T. Homan, *Middle Eastern Oil and the Western World*. American Elsevier, New York, 1971.

Shaw, John A., and David Long, *Saudi Arabian Modernization*. Praeger, New York, 1982.

Soffan, Londa Usra, *The Women of the United Arab Emirates*. Croom Helm, London, 1980.

St. Albans, Suzanne (The Duchess of St. Albans), *Where Time Stood Still: A Portrait of Oman*. Quartet Books, London, 1980.

Stewart, Desmond, *Mecca*. Newsweek Books, New York, 1980.

Stewart, Desmond, and the Editors of Time-Life Books, *Early Islam*. Time-Life Books, New York, 1967.

Stocking, George W., *Middle East Oil*. Vanderbilt University Press, Nashville, Tenn., 1970.

Thesiger, Wilfred, *Arabian Sands*. E. P. Dutton, New York, 1959.

Topham, John, Anthony Landreau and William

E. Mulligan, *Traditional Crafts of Saudi Arabia*. Stacey International, London, 1981.

Van Der Meulen, D., *The Wells of Ibn Saud*. Praeger, New York, 1957.

Vidal, F.S., *The Oasis of Al-Hasa*. Aramco, Washington, D.C., 1955.

Ward, Thomas E., *Negotiations for Oil Concessions in Bahrain, El Hasa (Saudi Arabia), The Neutral Zone, Qatar and Kuwait*. Private publication, 1965.

Wikan, Unni, *Behind the Veil in Arabia: Women in Oman*. The Johns Hopkins University Press, Baltimore, 1982.

Yorke, Valerie, *The Gulf in the 1980's*. Chatham House Papers. The Royal Institute of International Affairs, London, 1980.

PERIODICALS AND OTHER SOURCES

"Abu Dhabi's I Do's." *Time*, May 11, 1981.

"Emerging from the Dark Ages." *Time*, June 4, 1979.

Hourani, George F., "Did Competition Ruin South Arabia?" *Journal of Near Eastern Studies*, 1952.

"Inside Yemen." *Town and Country*, June 1983.

Journal of Energy and Development. International Research Center for Energy and Economic Development, Autumn 1979.

"Kuwait: Midas of the Persian Gulf." *Reader's Digest*, March 1981.

"Kuwaiti Broker Hits Record Books with $5.2 Billion." *The Washington Post*, May 30, 1983.

"Kuwait's Market Bailout." *The New York Times*, Feb. 18, 1983.

The Middle East. February, March, April 1982; February, March, April 1983.

Middle East Economic Digest. January, February, April 1983.

Middle East: North Africa. Review of Agriculture in 1981, U.S. Dept. of Agriculture.

"North Yemen." *National Geographic*, August 1979.

"Der Ol-Boom Macht die Beduinen Beqem." *GEO*, July 1980.

"Oman: In Dire Straits." *Newsweek*, Sept. 24, 1979.

"Third Development Plan, 1400-1405 A.H. (1980-1985)." Kingdom of Saudi Arabia, Ministry of Planning.

"Traders, Dealers, Survivors." *Time*, July 25, 1983.

"United Arab Emirates: A Record of Achievement, 1978-1981." The United Arab Emirates, Ministry of Information and Culture.

"Water Supply and Augmentation for the United Arab Emirates." U.S. Dept. of the Interior, Bureau of Reclamation, June 1979.

INDEX

Page numbers in italics refer to illustrations or illustrated text.

Colour separations by Scan Studio, Ltd., Dublin, Ireland.
Typesetting by Unwin Brothers Ltd., Woking, Surrey England
Printed in Spain by Artes Graficas Toledo S.A.

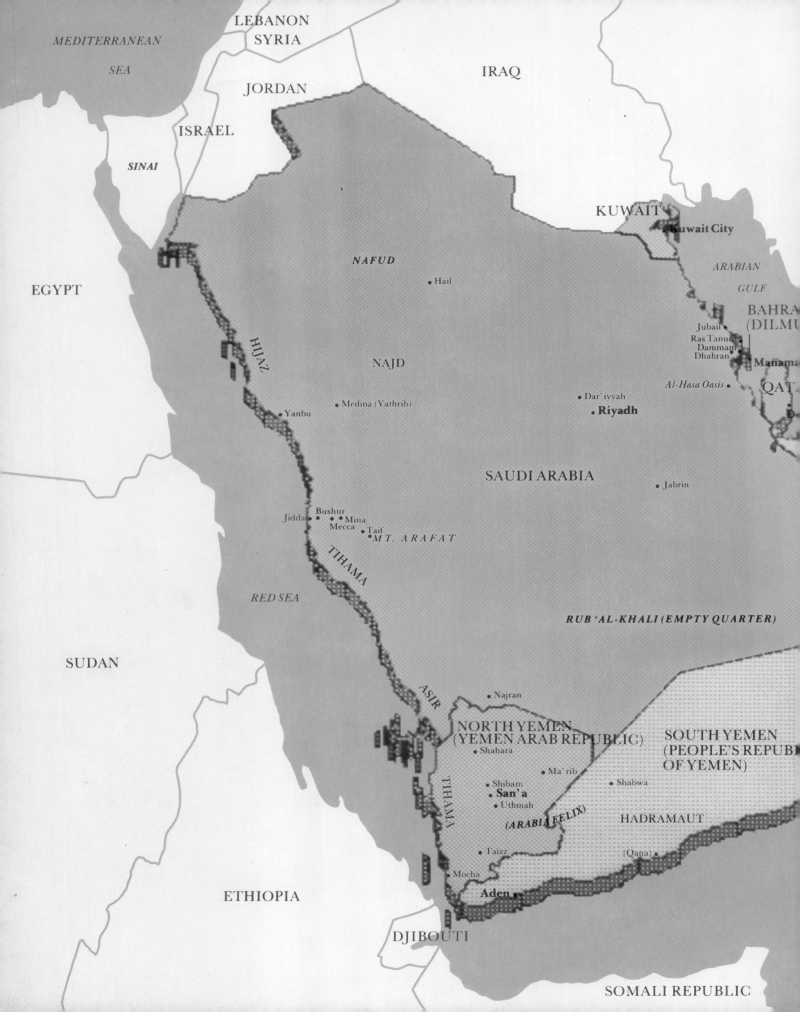